ONE MAN'S FAMILY

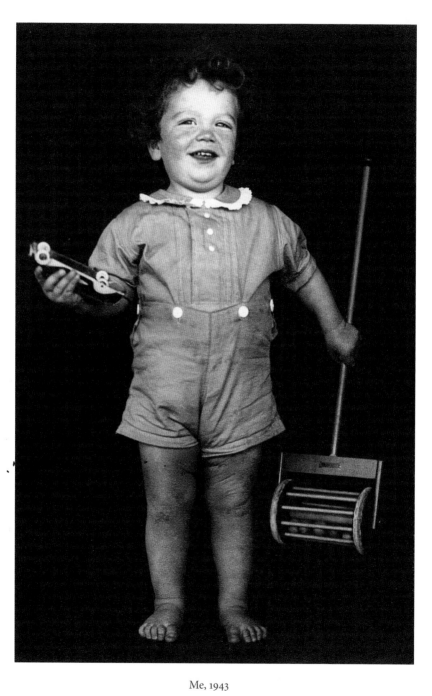

Me, 1943

July 18, 2014

ONE MAN'S FAMILY

Growing Up in Peterborough

~

SYDNEY M. WILLIAMS

Jane,

Fences don't make good
neighbors. Good neighbors
make good neighbors and,
Jane, you have been the
best good neighbor!
Sydney

Bauhan Publishing
Peterborough · New Hampshire
2014

ISBN: 978-0-87233-175-4

Library of Congress Cataloging-in-Publication Data

Williams, Sydney M. (Sydney Messer), 1941-
 One man's family : growing up in Peterborough / Sydney M. Williams.
  pages cm
Includes bibliographical references and index.
 ISBN 978-0-87233-175-4 (alkaline paper)
 1. Williams, Sydney M. (Sydney Messer), 1941—Childhood and youth.
 2. Williams, Sydney M. (Sydney Messer), 1941—Family. 3. Peterborough
 (N.H.)—Biography. 4. Peterborough (N.H.)—Social life and customs—
 20th century. 5. Families—New Hampshire—Peterborough—History—
 20th century. 6. Farm life—New Hampshire—Peterborough—History—
 20th century. 7. Skis and skiing—New Hampshire—Peterborough—
 History—20th century. I. Title.
 F44.P4W55 2014
 974.2'8043092—dc23
 [B]
                            2014015047

The cover drawing is by Sydney M. Williams, Jr. c. 1935, and used by permission.

The photograph on the front is reproduced on page 10 and identifies the Williams family.

The photographs and maps on pages 12, 23, 25 and 26 are courtesy of the Monadnock Center for Culture and History, Peterborough, New Hampshire and used by permission.

The photographs on pages 85 and 87 are by Joanna Eldredge Morrissey and used by permission.

The photograph of Stuart Williams' painting on page 80 is by Brianna Morrissey and used by permission.

All other photographs are from the Williams family and used by permission.

BAUHAN
PUBLISHINGLLC
PO BOX 117 PETERBOROUGH NEW HAMPSHIRE 03458
603-567-4430
WWW.BAUHANPUBLISHING.COM

Book design by Kirsty Anderson
Typeset in Minion Pro
Cover design by Henry James
Manufactured by Versa Press

Printed in the United States of America

To my Grandchildren

Caroline
Alex
Emma
Jack
Anna
Margaret
Henry
George
Sarah
Edith

Contents

FOREWORD

Truth is neither objectivity, nor the balanced view;
truth is a selfless subjectivity.

Knut Hamsun (1859–1952)
"Hunger" 1890

THE WORD "ESSAYS" IS TOO GRAND to describe these musings. They are reflections of a moment, a day or some period of time of my growing-up years. Some of them come forward to the present; others remain mired in the past. There is no particular order. They are random memories, studies, and reflections. There is a piece on my great-grand-parents. It is based on stories I heard and what I have since uncovered. I hope, in this collection, to catch a glimpse of a time gone by. We are all products of our particular past—genetically and geographically—influenced by the nature of those amongst whom we lived.

At the age of fifteen in the fall of 1956, I left home for boarding school. While Peterborough was still home, it would never be quite the same. As we live it, childhood seems to last forever. It is only when we are older that we realize how fleeting that time was. But, there is no question that we become who we are largely because of those early years. For good or for bad, one's early memories have a habit of sticking around more than most. It is not uncommon to hear someone my age being unable to recall what happened the day before, yet vividly recollect a schoolyard fight when he was eight. Another happy trick of nature is that the worst memories are generally erased, while happy ones remain firmly etched on our imaginations. (It is the fights we won, not those we lost, that are remembered.) Recently one of my sisters asked, what do I recall most fondly about growing up? My mind was filled with images and remembrances. When she asked what I liked least, a blank

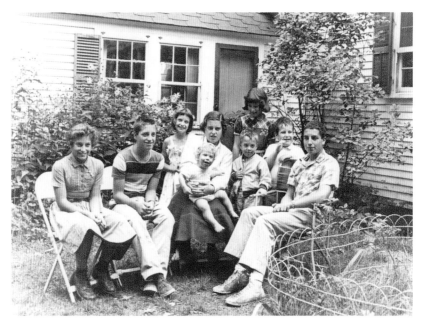

Left to right: Betsey, Frank, Jenny, Mary w/George, Charlotte, Willard, Stuart, me in 1956

slate appeared. It is not as though I were happy all the time. I cried and was upset on numerous occasions, but the instances and reasons have disappeared from memory—except for once when I was spanked for jumping into a flowerbed one Easter when I was about nine.

I am ever mindful of the extraordinary fortune that allowed me to come of age in this place and at that time. Reading history makes me realize how fortuitous it was that I came of age during a time of peace and prosperity in the United States. My parents did not, nor did their parents. War and the Depression intervened. Yet we also know that because of the miracle of our birth—the right sperm being introduced to the right egg—we could never have been born at a time different than we were. That knowledge, moreover, is what impels us to take full advantage of our time on earth.

It is my hope that you will take pleasure in this little book and that it will open a small window on a sliver of life lived in mid twentieth-century

My father and mother, East River, Connecticut, c. 1938

rural New Hampshire. More importantly, I hope it might tempt you to jot down your own memories. We learn best through our own experiences, but we can always learn something more through those of others.

The dozen or so short pieces collected here are not arranged chronologically, nor in the order in which they were originally written. The first two provide an overview. The next two deal with my parents. The rest follow somewhat haphazardly. I hope you enjoy them.

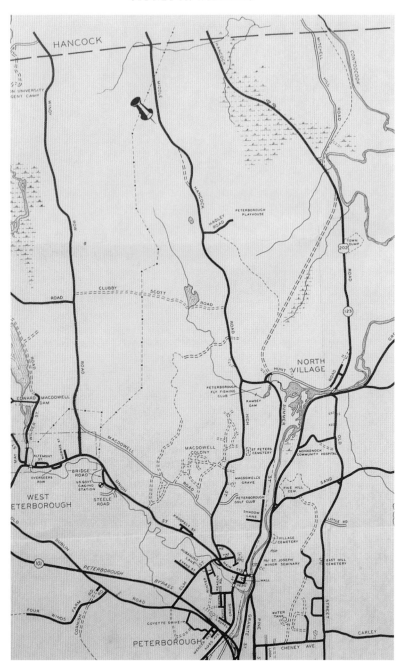

1944 map of Peterborough (courtesy of the Peterborough Historical Society)

A Tour of Past and Present

TWO OR THREE TIMES EACH YEAR my wife and I return to Peterborough, New Hampshire, typically staying at the nearby Hancock Inn, which has been operating continuously since 1789. To borrow a phrase, each visit is a trip down memory lane. Recently we drove from Hancock to Peterborough along the Middle Hancock Road, so named as it is the middle of three roads that run roughly parallel to each other. It was the road on which I grew up, with our house about midway between the two villages. In my mind, the road serves as a link tying the past to the present. Typical of New England landscapes, there is a church at either end of the road. When we drive the eight miles, I note what is that was, and am reminded of what was but is no more.

While the population of Hancock has almost tripled in the past sixty years to about 1,650 residents, Main Street is unchanged. At its eastern end, it begins at a fountain, a symbol of life, and culminates about half a mile to the west at the local cemetery, a place decorated with dozens of small American flags, commemorating the young people who have gone off to fight in every conflict since the French and Indian Wars began in 1754. Between the fountain and the cemetery are a dozen or so historic and well-kept homes. They are served by a post office, a meeting house that doubles as the Congregational Church, an inn, a library, the Hancock Historical Society, an insurance/real estate office, a small restaurant, and a general store. Across from the cemetery and just in back of the post office is Norway Pond, a spring-fed pond named for the Norway pines that line its banks; it is where my eight brothers and sisters and I learned to swim.

While we lived in Peterborough, our house was the last one before the Hancock town line, so we always felt ties to Hancock. Besides swimming, every year we would ride the four miles to the village on horseback to participate in the town's Old Home Day Parade, typically held in mid August. Additionally, my parents had many friends in the town—Miss Perry and Pat Holsart; the Lloyd Briggs family; Bob English, his

Jenny at the Old Home Day Parade, c. 1954

father-in-law Joseph Grew, and his son Joe, a few years older than me.

My paternal grandfather owned 900 acres on a place called Cobb's Hill, land he bought for less than a dollar an acre around 1910. The land is now owned by the Conservation Trust and includes the Cobb Hill Trail operated by the Harris Trust Center. On the land in the old days was a tumbled-down structure called the Jaquith house (named after the former owner), where as a young man, my father would camp out with friends, and where years later we would pick blackberries and picnic. The road beyond it was barely passable during my youth.

The village of Hancock sits on a ridge, and the road to Peterborough dips sharply down at the start. Near the bottom, on the left, is a house that belonged to Mme. de Pierrefeu, an older woman whom my parents knew. Mme. de Pierrefeu believed in the ability to communicate with the dead. As I remember it my parents were once at her home for a séance. My mother, never a believer in the occult, apparently yawned, and was urged by her hostess to retire to the next room for a nap. Never abashed or embarrassed, Mama did so, or at least that is how I recall the story.

At the foot of the hill is a house we knew well when it belonged to Hugh and Dorothy Palmer. It is a Cape with naturally weathered shingles that have darkened with age, and is hidden by trees, with a small brook behind. Allegedly, it had been moved from Cobb's Hill. As such, it was a reminder of the devastating effect the opening of the Ohio Valley had upon small New England farmers. Train service, which allowed the Midwest to boom, tolled death for New Hampshire farmers whose rocky fields could not compete with the wide open spaces of the Ohio River region. The Palmers' house and several others were taken down and brought to the village when the farms they owned were no longer viable. It was an early and real example of Joseph Schumpeter's theory of "creative destruction."

The Palmers were between my parents and grandparents in age, and there was always a tinge of mystery about them. While we were not related, we called them, at their insistence, Auntie Dot and Uncle Hugh. Mr. Palmer had graduated from West Point and was still serving as an army officer when we first knew him, generally in some educational role. When he was older and had retired, he took a job as head of a small, private school in Greenwich, Connecticut, located where the Eagle Hill School now is. We often stopped at the Palmers' house in Hancock when returning from a swim in Norway Pond, or in one of Hancock's two larger ponds: Willard Pond or Nubanusit Lake. We were always assured of a glass of lemonade, a cookie, and the opportunity to play with Mr. Palmer's collection of cast-iron mechanical banks.

During the first couple of years of World War II, my father took a job working on Miss Perry's farm, about four miles away. Miss Perry was a granddaughter of Admiral Perry who opened Japan. She lived on a dirt road known as the Old Dublin Road, about two miles from the Palmers. Because of war-time gas rationing, my father went back and forth by horse and buggy. He would frequently stop at the Palmers' for lemonade. When he left for home, he knew that the horse, Nona, could find the way, so he would prop up his feet and read all the way back.

We may believe that we live in an age unique for its ability to communicate. But small towns in the 1940s offered extraordinary services. My parents were once at dinner with the Palmers when the phone rang. The call was for my mother; it was from her mother in Madison, Connecticut. The switchboard operator in Peterborough received the call and, knowing that my parents were dining with the Palmers, simply called their house. It beat call-forwarding and obviated cell phones!

Continuing along the road, we passed what was once Mrs. John D. Peabody's place, Valley Farm. When we were young, the farm was owned by Sidney Stearns and his wife. Mrs. Peabody, whose first name was Mary, bought the place sometime later after the death of her husband. She and her husband had owned a dairy farm in Massachusetts. Like a lot of transplants, she had her oddities, including a cook who had once served time in prison. She had conservative beliefs and would refer to herself as a "New York" Peabody, to differentiate herself from another Mary Peabody, the mother of Endicott Peabody and a civil rights heroine of the early 1960s. The Hancock Mrs. Peabody was a fervent believer in prayer in school. In 1963, after the Supreme Court prohibited the state sponsorship of prayer in public schools, she protested the action by blocking the entrance to the local school. A few years later, my brother Willard worked for her. One of his jobs was to drive her to the school where she would sneak into a classroom to conduct prayers. Her daughter, curiously, married the brother of one of my wife's best friends. (I say "curiously" because my wife grew up in New York City, a world away from rural New Hampshire.)

The Middle Hancock Road, which was dirt in my earliest memories, continues. About a mile further on is a well-maintained gray Cape. The house belonged to the Turpins, of whom I have no memory, although I believe his first name was Senath, a name unusual even in New Hampshire. Earlier and more famously, it was the childhood home of Haydn S. Pearson, who came to Glenrose Farm with his family, including his minister father, in 1908, when he (Haydn) was seven. When I was growing up, Mr. Pearson was a columnist for one of the Boston papers and lived in Greenfield, New Hampshire, a town just to the east. He had

View outside our house to Crotched Mountain

written several books, a number of them on cooking, like *The Country-man's Cookbook* and *Country Flavor,* but my favorite was *That Darned Minister's Son.* It is a story of his childhood and a book sadly out of print, but which I own and often re-read. One of my favorite stories recounted the time when, about age ten, he fired a spitball at his father who was preaching his weekly sermon. Needless to say, this being a time when disrespect for one's elders did not go unpunished, his father interrupted his sermon to attend to his son. A few minutes later a chastened boy, holding back tears, returned to his pew, and his father, satisfied with having punished a sinner, completed his sermon.

Just past the Turpin/Pearson house, the road dips and then rises to where Windy Row goes off to the right. The Putnams lived on the corner; their house burned when I was about twelve. My brother Frank, aged about ten, happened to be on his way to visit a friend when he passed the burning house. That, of course, made me jealous. It was the witnessing of a fire—not concern for the family or their possessions—that captured my interest. A new house now sits where the Putnams once lived, and the view is beautiful—Crotched Mountain rising to the east with North Pack Monadnock just to its south—though there are more trees today than when I was young. In fact, a hundred and more years ago there were fields on both sides of the road, lined with stone walls built from the granite that give New Hampshire its nickname, "the Granite State."

About a half mile further was the home of Mr. and Mrs. Charles Adams. They were closer in age to my grandparents, and I recall Mr. Adams keeping one field at a remove from the others and invisible from the road—a place he could work on Sundays, which would have been in violation of New Hampshire's (or Hancock's) "blue laws." Blue laws date back to an earlier time, when church and state were more closely intertwined. Inertia has kept some of those laws on the books. Even as recently as three years ago there was a law (unenforced) that no person shall "engage in any play, game or sport" on Sundays. Mr. Adams served for a while as a selectman for the town of Hancock. The town report for 1943 showed his annual expenses as selectman had been $35.27. (Pennies were distinctly more cherished seventy years ago than today.) The Adams had one daughter, Anna Mae, who served as our babysitter when we were quite young, but who shortly thereafter moved to Chicago. Today, with her husband Dr. Daniel L. Wallace, who retired as a professor of statistics at the University of Chicago, she spends summers at the farm. When I was a child their kitchen always smelled wonderfully of freshly baked pies and donuts, straight out of the oven of a wood-stoked stove. Mrs. Adams' brother had a seat on the New York Stock Exchange, a fact that always seemed at odds with his sister enjoying life without indoor plumbing.

Another half mile and the road passes by Mr. Lindsley's weekend home. Thayer Lindsley, the son of missionaries, was born and brought up in Japan. He studied geology and staked out, among other finds, the Falconbridge Nickel Mines outside of Sudbury, Ontario. Franklin Delano Roosevelt was his roommate freshman year at Harvard. Mr. Lindsley claimed he did not like FDR then and liked him even less as time went on. Mr. Lindsley had homes in New York, Toronto, and Paris, and so always had a cosmopolitan aura. He was a believer in the mystical attraction of fairies (or *faeries*, as he would have spelled the word)—not the storybook ones we think of today, but real ones that lived in forests, under leaves, and who could perform feats of magic. In the summer of 1961 I worked in a smelter at the Falconbridge mines. And the summer before, I worked for him as a prospector for the Nahanni Syndicate, which was doing some exploratory work in Canada's Northwest Territories along the Yukon border. His home was endlessly fascinating, filled with Asian trinkets and treasures. Living on the Peterborough-Hancock line and being our closest neighbor to the north, Mr. Lindsley was someone we saw frequently when he was at home in New Hampshire.

The road crosses a brook marking the town line. During the Hurricane of 1938, the brook overflowed and the road washed out. The road was not fully repaired until after the war. Today, as during my childhood, it ascends quite steeply to a ridge where, when leaves are off the trees, one gets another view of Crotched Mountain and North and Pack Monadnocks. The road heading back toward Hancock was a wonderful place to coast on sleds when ice and snow provided cover. It sloped down for about a quarter of a mile, so we could pick up some pretty good speed. I recall once loading the new Methodist minister, fresh from Texas, onto our bobsled, giving him a scare that probably made him wonder why he ever left his home state.

Our house came next. It had been known as the Dodge Place and sits on the west side of the road, about a quarter of a mile from the top of the hill. (It is described in more detail in the next essay.)

Just south of us was a place we called the "brick house," which is now the home of the Well School. Sixty years ago the place was empty, but owned by a family named Yelland. In one of the fields, where in June we would pick strawberries, sat an abandoned Model A roadster, in which I would sit and pretend to be driving off to distant lands and great adventures. Across the road but invisible from the brick house, was a new house built by Dick Noyes in the 1950s. He had grown up in Peterborough and was a Navy pilot in the Japanese theater during World War II.

During the mid 1950s he began publication of a paper that became *The Monadnock Ledger,* providing competition to the *Peterborough Transcript.* Both papers were weeklies. Ultimately, but after Mr. Noyes had sold the paper, the *Ledger* bought the *Transcript.* Dick Noyes did not live there long as he and his wife kept having children and the house was small. It was sold to Emily Dusser de Barenne, a friend of my parents, who moved to Peterborough as a widow. The world was small even in that distant time: Her brother, Dr. Daniel C. Greene of Baltimore, had been a classmate of my father at Harvard.

About half a mile further on was a collection of two or three farms. They are still there, but no longer function as farms. The first was the Flaggs' place. Around 1948, Orrin Flagg sold the big house and barn to the Lobackis, who raised chickens. He built a smaller house, mostly by hand when in his eighties. Mr. Flagg was born about 1859. He served in New Hampshire's militia, which took him to Concord, the state's capital and the furthest he ever went from home. Their daughter Margaret was the second grade teacher in Peterborough.

Just beyond was a compound of Naglies. The grandfather, Jim, with his wife and two sons, Frank and Ken, lived in three houses. Ken and his wife had three children who became our friends—Lillie Mae, Jim, and Earle. My first paying job was bringing the half-dozen cows that had spent the day grazing in the field across the road from our house— "Naglie's pasture," as we called it—back to Jim Naglie's barn. He paid me, as I recall, a quarter a day for the job. (It may have been for a week.) It was in a field behind Ken Naglie's house that I smoked my first cigar, an experience that kept me off them for many years. It was also from that same field that I once threw a snowball which, with unerring aim, entered the window of a passing car and smacked the driver in the head. After threatening to take me to the police station for a chat with Mr. Picard, the police chief, the driver thought better and let me go. Driving past the Naglies' place today, it looks smaller and sadder than I remembered.

After grandfather Naigle died in the mid 1950s, his house was bought by Barbara and Francis Golffing, she a poet and he a professor at Franklin Pierce College in Rindge, New Hampshire. Mrs. Golffing, a Stanford graduate, wrote poetry under the name Barbara Gibbs and received a Guggenheim Fellowship in 1955. Professor Golffing was born in Vienna in 1910. He, along with thousands of others, was forced out by the Nazis and moved to this country in 1941. My brother Willard noted that my father often commented on the resulting wonderful juxtaposition of neighbors.

Just beyond the Naglies' is the cut-off to the Peterborough Players. Edith Bond Stearns began the theater in 1933, in the depths of the Depression. She purchased an abandoned place known as the Hadley farm that had no electricity or running water, which was not particularly uncommon in those days in rural New Hampshire. By late summer the theater was in operation, with *Manikin and Minikin* being their first production. The show had had a one-night run on Broadway in 1927. (Mrs. Stearns' son Johnny began his career in the mid 1920s at the Mariarden Theater, about a mile south on Middle Hancock Road. Johnny Stearns went on to fame as half of the duo in one of TV's earliest sitcoms, *Mary Kay and Johnny*.) The 1920s into the early 1950s was a golden period for summer theaters. For hundreds of actors, such as Roxanna Cox and James Whitmore, summer stock productions provided an opportunity to practice their craft in pleasant surroundings. While no one made much money, the expenses were not high. My parents were subscribers and I remember many enjoyable performances. The Peterborough Players is still going strong today. The 2013 season, which lasts from early June to early October, included seven shows, among them *Say Goodnight, Gracie; Absurd Person Singular;* and *Tea for Three.* The modernized theater-barn now seats 250 people. Indicative of a changing population, my brother Frank told me he recently attended a show and saw no one he knew.

Continuing toward Peterborough, the road passes what we used to call the "bear house," a tumbling shack alongside of the road. As children, we would scare ourselves into believing the place was appropriately named. The shack is still there, but any bears have departed. Just beyond on the left, in what was once a sandpit, is a new home. I remember catching frogs in one of the small ponds nearby, frying their legs on the Naglies' stove for a midday snack. A great uncle to the Naglie children built a sap house on that land. On the right was another sandpit where a young man a few years younger than I committed suicide.

The road ascends a hill, again with great views of Crotched Mountain to the east, across from where the Balchs once lived, and then dips down to a home that was owned by the Westovers, on the west side of the road. The Balchs were grandparents to the Westover boys, both of whom were older than I. One son, Wayne, I knew slightly. The older son, Dean, was born in 1934 and developed some fame as an aviator. He wrote a book recently about his experiences, *Final Approach*. Their home was on land adjacent to what was once the Mariarden Theater School.

The name of the acting school likely derived from the maiden name of William Shakespeare's mother, Mary Arden. While it closed before I was born, it ran from about 1920 to 1934 as a dance and drama school, with special emphasis on dance and Shakespeare. Martha Graham danced there in the early 1920s. In 1924 Paul Robeson played the title role in Eugene O'Neill's *The Emperor Jones*. This was where Bette Davis, at the age of sixteen, received her early training. She was cast in Shakespeare's *As You Like It* and *A Midsummer's Night Dream*. Other notables who got their start at Mariarden were dancers Ruth St. Denis and Ted Shawn. Kay Brown Barrett, who became known for acquiring *Gone with the Wind* for David Selznick, had her first job there. The theater has been recognized as one of the first (if not *the* first) professional outdoor theaters in the United States. Its outdoor amphitheater could seat 600. Interestingly, it was half-owned by Joseph Kennedy, father of President John F. Kennedy. If one is very rich and has an eye for beautiful women, what better than a school where you can house, display, and visit them? Peterborough is seventy-five miles from Boston, close enough to visit, yet far enough to be discrete.

Next on the right was the home of Robb Sagendorph, founder and

The barn studio at Mariarden (courtesy of the Peterborough Historical Society)

publisher of *Yankee Magazine.* In 1939, he acquired the rights to *The Old Farmer's Almanac,* which survives to this day. Its claim to fame is its weather forecast. The road then goes down what we called Pettengill's Hill, with the Pettengills' house at the bottom. Getting stuck on the steep hill with its turn at the bottom, became a regular part of life on slick winter days. The descending road then passes the Fly Pond, which today looks very small, but always seemed adequate for a pick-up hockey game when we were young. I recall, when I was about twelve, interrupting a hockey game to watch the truck go by with the carcass of Nona, the horse who took my father back and forth to his job at Miss Perry's. As the ground was frozen, no grave could be dug; Nona was being trucked to Benson's Wild Animal Farm in Hudson, New Hampshire. It was, of course, an early example of recycling: Nona's last gift would be to serve as supper for the lions.

At this point, the road heading toward Peterborough follows the Contoocook River as it flows north. About a mile from the village more houses begin to appear. Mr. Russell, known to all of us as "Dirty Joe," had a shack alongside the river on the left. A little further on was a collection of small houses, one of which was home to the Tatreaus, and another to the seven Sangermano children, the younger of whom were around my age. Across the street on the right, where Whit's Tow had been, is the Heritage Apartments complex. Howard Whitcomb loomed large in my young life. Whit's Tow was where I learned to ski in the post-war years. A rope tow carried skiers up a hill to the golf course. Sometime in the 1950s, Mr. Whitcomb built a trail to the right of the main tow, which we dubbed "Suicide," as it went straight down for a "hair-raising" fifty feet! To the far right was a children's slope where we first learned to ski. Ann Eneguess was one of our early instructors, though I recall my father just putting us on skis and assuming we would take naturally to the sport.

As we approach the village, we drive by what was once a nursing home on the right. Across the street and next to the locker plant used to be a small orphanage. I remember the school bus stopping in front of the orphanage, where two or three young children got on. The locker plant was where, before household freezers became common, people could keep food items frozen. The first home ice-boxes were just that—a wooden cabinet lined, I believe, with lead. We used one until 1953. Once a week my mother would drive to the local ice-man and have a block placed in the car. Once home, we placed the ice in one of the lower drawers of the ice box where it would keep items such as milk and eggs cool.

Middle Hancock Road terminates at Main Street in Peterborough, with the Unitarian (now Unitarian-Universalist) church on the right and what was once a gas station on the left. The church is the place where my sisters were married and where the burial services for my parents and two siblings were conducted.

Driving from Hancock to Peterborough along the Middle Hancock Road is indeed like taking a trip through the past. It reminds me that no matter how much things change, there is much that lasts.

Peterborough today is almost three times the size it was when I was

Looking up Main Street in downtown Peterborough, c. 1940

growing up, yet the sense of the village center seems little changed. The movie theater and railroad station are gone, as are the two drugstores and Derby's department store, all of which I remember so well. There are shopping malls outside the village. The town is more yuppified, and probably not as intimate as it once was. One of the larger stores is now my brother Willard's bookstore, The Toadstool, which, in a world of big-box stores and electronic reading tablets, continues to prosper, thanks to Willard's hands-on management. Yet the intersection of Grove and Main Streets, with the town hall on the southwest corner looks unchanged, and the town is still home to a diverse and interesting group of people.

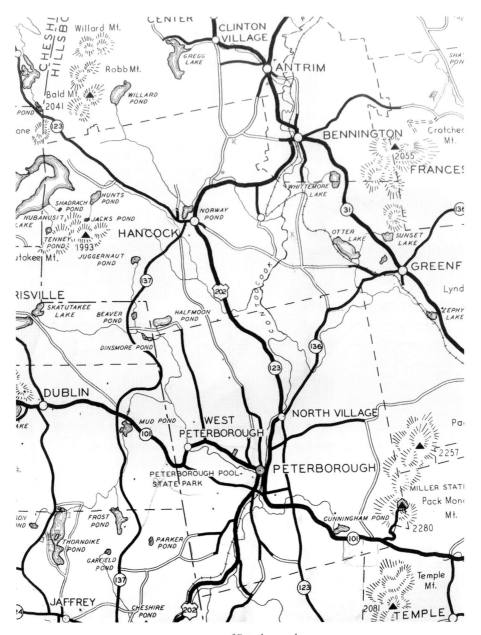

1944 map of Peterborough

Peterborough, New Hampshire, in the 1940s and '50s

So we beat on, boats against the current, borne back ceaselessly into the past.
F. Scott Fitzgerald (1896–1940)
The Great Gatsby, 1925

*Just specimens is all New Hampshire has, one each of everything
as in a show-case which naturally she doesn't care to sell.*
Robert Frost (1874–1963)
"New Hampshire"
New Hampshire, 1923

LIKE A PACK RAT, MY MOTHER SAVED and hoarded letters, drawings, photos, and other remnants from an earlier time. Like her, I have done the same. There are a couple of dozen letters and half a dozen telegrams heralding my birth: "Am thrilled to hear about the little boy;" "Can't wait to see you and your son;" "Three cheers for Sydney." It's pretty heady stuff, even from a distance of seventy-plus years. While there is so much promise in each new life, there must have been many times when my parents wondered at God's purpose for mine. Nevertheless, there are myriad reminders of my early years. There is a collection of drawings I did when I was five or six years old, packed away in manila folders. There is an Easter postcard from my father from 1945 when he was serving in Italy; *Buona Pasqua* is printed on the front with a depiction of three elves, each carrying a large egg; on the reverse is written, "Dear Sydney, I wonder if you'll find any Easter eggs as big as these. Love, Papa." There are thousands of photographs. One pictures me as a newborn held lovingly and gently by my father. Another depicts me struggling in the arms of my great-grandmother. A third photo, taken a few years later, shows a scene outside the kitchen door in Peterborough: Judy, one of the horses, is hitched to a sledge on which lies a freshly cut spruce. My father holds the reins. Around are sprinkled Mama and six of us children; Stuart, born three weeks earlier, is not in the photo. It is Christmas Eve 1950. That evening my father would light real candles to adorn the tree—with a bucket of water placed within easy reach. These photos, letters, and drawings provide a vital connection to my early years. While we live in the present and prepare for the future, we are products of the past. Genetics and environment together determine who we become.

HOME

The farm where I grew up was known as the Dodge Place, named after a family who lived there and conducted a small business making mercury-filled thermometers in the late nineteenth and very early twentieth centuries. My paternal grandparents bought the place as part of a larger property around 1915. When my parents moved to the farm in 1938 shortly after they were married, it was still known as the Dodge Place and was called that throughout my early years. Rooting around in the dirt near the house, my brother Frank and I often came across, and played with, pieces of mercury left behind forty or more years earlier. Despite later warnings about the devastation that mercury can cause, we never suffered any ill effects.

The house sat on about 150 acres of the rocky soil so well known to New Hampshire farmers. My parents, who had become sculptors, had been raised in privileged surroundings—my mother in New Haven and Madison, Connecticut, and my father in Wellesley, Massachusetts, and Peterborough, New Hampshire—but this was nine years into a Depression that seemed without end. The Dodge Place was adjacent to, and a little over a mile from, my father's parents' summer home. That is, it was a little over a mile via an old logging road that passed through the woods, but about six miles by car. (I recall once, not long after World War II, watching my grandparents emerge from the woods in their Oldsmobile.)

The place was four miles from the village, which at that time was a

Our barn, c. 1938

town of about 2,500. The house, the size of which must have been comfortable when my parents moved in as newlyweds in their late twenties, seemed to grow progressively smaller as children kept arriving. With the exception of eighteen months during World War II, they would live there while raising nine children for the next thirty years.

THE TOWN

The first white settlers came to what is now Peterborough in 1738, occupying land that had been hunted by the Penacooks, a member tribe of the Algonquins. Today it is a village of some 6,000 and is the commercial center of the eight towns that abut it—Harrisville, Hancock, Greenfield, Lyndeborough, Temple, Sharon, Jaffrey, and Dublin. The town sits at the juncture of two highways, U.S. Routes 202 and 101, and at the point where the Nubanusit River flows into the Contoocook—a north-flowing river that merges with the Merrimac River and continues onward to

Peterborough Railroad Depot, c. 1940

empty into the Atlantic Ocean at Newburyport, Massachusetts.

When I was growing up in the late 1940s and early 1950s, Peterborough still had regular rail service. The Monadnock Railroad Company first provided rail service to Peterborough in 1871. While the rail tracks north of town were washed out during the Hurricane of 1938, and never replaced, trains continued to come to the Peterborough station for another fifteen years. During my early years passenger and freight trains arrived once a day. My maternal grandmother used to visit by train. She would travel from New Haven to Springfield, change trains for Worcester and then change again for Peterborough. The last passenger train to leave the Peterborough station departed on March 7, 1953, at 2:05p.m., and I was on it. Two hundred and forty-eight people boarded the train for this historic final departure. Most of us got off in the next town, Jaffrey.

There were two grocery stores in town, the IGA and Lloyd's; two drugstores; a hardware store; Derby's, a department store; a movie theater, in which the films were changed three times a week; Steele's, a variety store where comic books could be bought; a feed store adjacent to the depot; a couple of banks; assorted auto dealers, the largest being Nichol's Ford Agency, tucked behind the Peterborough Tavern; and six or seven churches, one Catholic and the rest a variety of Protestant denominations, including the Unitarian Church, a beautiful and centrally located edifice. The Peterborough Tavern served as an inn for travelers and dated back to stagecoach days. We bought our gas at O'Malley's, skied at Whit's Tow, and read the *Peterborough Transcript,* printed every Thursday. Albert "Del" Picard was the chief of police and knew every teenager in town. New Hampshire Ball Bearings, the largest employer in town, and The Noone Mills, just south of the village, provided factory work.

The most imposing building in Peterborough was the Main Street headquarters of the Guernsey Cattle Club, which had been recently (and surprisingly) relocated from Iowa. The population was virtually all Caucasian and generally Protestant—and still is—though there was a large contingent of French-Canadian Catholics, most of whom lived in West Peterborough and worked for the Verney textile factory, which produced rayon parachute cloth and subsequently closed, or moved south, after the end of World War II. The one Jewish family in town, the Goldmans, owned one of the two drugstores and their presence contributed to what little the town had in terms of ecumenicalism. It was, at that time, a strongly Republican town. The MacDowell Colony, the Peterborough Players, and the Sharon Arts Center provided artistic stimulation, and were all run by friends of my family.

Geographically the town is in southwest New Hampshire, about twenty miles from the Massachusetts border. It is bounded on the east by Crotched Mountain and North and Pack Monadnocks, and on the southwest by Mount Monadnock, perhaps the most-climbed treeless summit in the United States. From its peak on a clear day, one can see the harbor at Boston, seventy-five miles to the south and east. To the south is the Contoocook Valley; to the north and west the land slopes gently higher. While taller, steeper, and more rugged, the Apennines, which my father saw as an infantryman during World War II, reminded him of the hills around Peterborough.

A LITTLE FAMILY HISTORY

During the late nineteenth and early twentieth centuries, summer visitors were drawn to the Peterborough area by the beauty of the rolling hills, lakes, and streams, the majesty of Mount Monadnock, and the region's proximity to Boston. My paternal grandparents were part of that migration, arriving in 1910, the year my father was born.

My father's mother was raised in Boston and Wellesley, Massachusetts, in very comfortable surroundings. Her father, as a recent Harvard graduate, had accompanied Louis Agassiz on the Thayer Expedition to the Amazon in 1865. She inherited his interest in the natural world and spent several years studying at M.I.T., but was refused a degree because of her gender. Her husband, my grandfather, was born in Taunton, Massachusetts, into a family of educators. For two years, following his graduation from Harvard in 1894, he taught French at Milton Academy before becoming a bond broker. Several years later, with the prospect of marrying into a wealthy family, he wrote his bride-to-be, "For several years I have helped my aunt and my sister. . . . Last year, on account of the panic [the letter is undated, but I presume he is referring to the Panic of 1907], the firm's profits amounted to practically nothing; so living expenses took the two or three thousand that I had saved up to that time. Today, therefore, I've nothing but a *probable* income of $2,500 to $3,000, and an optimistic disposition." One wonders, in similar circumstances, how such a letter would be received today? While they wintered in Wellesley, in the house in which my grandmother had been born, Peterborough offered a place away from the confines of the family compound, and one my grandfather could truly call his own. My father had spent every summer there and, during winter holidays, he had often brought a group of his Harvard friends for cross-country skiing tours in the nearby hills. It provided a wonderful venue for a growing family.

My maternal grandfather was a banker-industrialist from an old New Haven family, and my maternal grandmother, who had grown up on a large tobacco farm in central Tennessee and in Washington, D.C., was the daughter of a U.S. congressman. My mother graduated from the Foxcroft School and then studied sculpture with William Boni in Rome before returning to Middleburg, Virginia, where she taught art at her *alma mater* for two years. The fraud and subsequent collapse of Ivar Kreuger and his financial empire in early 1932, which included most famously the Swedish Match Company, caused considerable financial losses for my maternal grandfather. He had considered Ivar Kreuger a friend (Kreuger visited the family home) and had invested heavily in his enterprises, both personally and as a director of the Irving Trust Company. On the mantle of our home in Peterborough was a silver cigarette holder which, as my mother would point out, was the sole asset my grandfather recovered from that fraud[1]. He had to give up retirement. He became president of the Cambridge Rubber Company, but the house in New Haven, an Italianate brownstone, had to be sold. (It is now owned by Yale University.) They moved full time to Madison, Connecticut, to their home, "Wyndham."

THE HOUSE, BARN, AND PROPERTY

My parents met in 1937 as students of George Demetrios, a sculptor with studios in Boston and Gloucester, Massachusetts. They were married a year later and, after a short honeymoon, moved to the Dodge Place on my grandparents' property.

The house was built around 1825, probably as a Cape. It had been expanded with an ell and a second floor. The house faced east and was

---

1 The story of Ivar Kreuger deserves a little more elaboration, especially following our recent period of credit concerns, for the Kreuger scam, in current dollar terms, was the biggest financial fraud ever committed. Kreuger returned to Sweden in 1907 at age twenty-seven, after having spent considerable time in the United States, and set up a construction business, Kreuger & Toll. Shortly afterwards he assumed control of his grandfather's match factory. In 1913 he formed a trust to consolidate the industry and to control all aspects of match production, including pulp and paper mills. His financial acumen allowed him to expand into other businesses such as telecommunications and mining. By 1929 he was producing 40 percent of the world's matches, and his holdings included Diamond matches in the United States. By the late 1920s he was making loans to needy European governments still suffering the consequences of World War I, in return for monopoly rights. By 1930, Kreuger had provided $350 million to a dozen countries still suffering the effects of World War I, and was known as "the savior of Europe." Much of the financing for his enterprises (including the loans he was making to foreign governments) came from the United States, and when the U.S. stock markets crashed, his financial weaknesses were revealed. In 1931, short of cash, he apparently forged some Italian government bonds. Rather than face his creditors, he committed suicide in his Paris apartment on March 12, 1932.

After four years of attempts to straighten out the financial mess, Price Waterhouse determined that between the years 1917 and 1932, Kreuger overstated his earnings by $250 million. Most of the remaining assets were ultimately acquired by Jacob Wallenberg for just $15 million. The Swedish Match Company survives today, having had a number of different owners (including Volvo, which spun it off to shareholders in 1996), and trades publicly on the Stockholm exchange.

The "Dodge Place," our home, c. 1938

set back about a hundred feet from the road, with a row of lilacs for separation. The ell extended toward the rear and housed the stairwell, a dining room, two pantries, the kitchen, a shed, and a wood shed. The front part, facing the road, included the living room and what we called the "end room," a room into which were dumped works of art (completed and in-progress), unused wedding gifts, and the like. As children, it was a room we rarely entered. Upstairs were four bedrooms and two bathrooms. Two of the bedrooms and both bathrooms were above the ell, all facing south off a long, narrow hallway, while my parents' room was above the living room. A large, screened-in sleeping porch faced north off the hallway. At the far end of the hallway, above the shed, was the fourth bedroom, a room we called the "purple room," which was generally reserved in early days for guests, especially my maternal grandparents.

There was no central heat (insulation wasn't added until about 1950) a coal-burning furnace provided hot water for the taps and the radiators

The Peterborough elementary school, in the 1940s

in the bathrooms. "Air conditioning" was achieved by opening windows. A woodstove in the kitchen served both as heat in the winter and a place to cook year round. A second woodstove in the dining room and a fireplace in the living room provided heat in those areas. Until 1953, an ice chest in the shed off the kitchen was the only source of refrigeration, and a lone, hand-crank telephone was located in the stairwell. The telephone line was a party line, meaning we shared it with a half-dozen other families. (Snooping on neighbors was frowned upon, but often too tempting to resist.) Our ring on this party line was three "longs" and two "shorts."

CHILDHOOD MEMORIES

At the time my parents moved in, the road was dirt; the Hurricane of 1938 blew through a few months after they arrived and washed out the road a half mile to the north. So for the first few years they lived at the end of a dirt road, but as I remember it, the road was paved and the wash-out repaired.

My earliest memories are of staying with my maternal grandparents at Wyndham in East River, Connecticut, the westernmost part of the town of Madison. It was a wonderful house, on the beach but with plenty of land and a barn. When my father was drafted into the Army in March of 1944, my mother, pregnant with my sister Betsy, returned to her parents' home with three children, a couple of goats, two dogs, and a cat or two in tow. I had just turned three. There were always plenty of fresh eggs and we were raised on goat's milk. Shortly after we arrived, my mother acquired a Shetland pony. My memories are spotty and few: my older sister, Mary, dressing me in a jumper and Mary Jane shoes; my sister Betsy's arrival in August; playing on the beach in front of the house; my father's departure for overseas duty in September; Christmas that year and a red fire engine I received; and the death of Julius the gardener.

Near the end of July 1945, we returned to Peterborough. My father was expected to be home on leave for a month before being shipped to Japan for the invasion anticipated for that fall. As it turned out, he arrived on the fifteenth of August, V-J Day. Images of that day are etched in my memory—my father coming toward us, having gotten off the troop train; horns blaring and car lights flashing. We all knew there would be no invasion and the long war was over.

⁓

What I remember best about our home in Peterborough was the activity. As I got older and sought solitude, I would take to the woods on foot, horseback, or skis, but it was the noise—the talk, laughter, crying—that pervaded the place both inside and out that I remember best. Likewise, the barn hummed: horses stamping their feet and neighing; goats leaping and bleating; chickens clucking and scurrying. My father enjoyed inventing and playing with names for them. Our first rabbit was named "Peter." The second became "Repeat." A tom cat he named "Henry" and

Me and Frank, July 4, 1952

when Henry was joined by a female, my father named her "Henrietta." A third cat became "Gladiator."

~

Births and deaths provided a cadence for the years between my father's return from Italy and my departure for boarding school eleven years later. Five more children were born: Charlotte in 1946, Jenny in 1948, Stuart in 1950, Willard in 1952, and George in 1955. Dogs and cats were born, died, and replaced. The first two horses my parents owned (they were previously owned by my paternal grandparents), Nona and Jill, died during those years. Mitzi, a Shetland pony bought by my mother in Connecticut, was soon joined by Judy—half Thoroughbred and half workhorse—and, a couple of years later, by Winnie, a Welsh pony, who was a gift from the headmistress of my mother's school. Winnie, who became my pony, was bred to an Arabian stallion and foaled Star, a lively filly who became Frank's. Additional horses arrived over the years. The goat herd increased to about ten and we always had a dozen chickens, a few ducks, and a couple of rabbits. Two peacocks, a gift from my mother's oldest brother, arrived in the early 1950s; I can still hear the eerie, almost-human shrillness of their calls.

Many recollections of those days pop into my mind at odd moments. A person, an activity, a place triggers a memory. Once, in about 1951, we were driving in our secondhand 1941 Ford station wagon, headed for my grandmother's place in East River to spend a few weeks. The car was loaded with luggage and laden with seven children (Willard and George were yet unborn) and assorted dogs and cats, and we hauled a trailer housing a pony and a few goats. We pulled into a gas station near

Belchertown, Massachusetts. The attendant came out, surveyed the car and the trailer, and queried, "Where are you heading?"

"To my mother's," replied my mother.

"Does she know you're coming?" he asked laconically.

My parents laughed.

~

At the age of three, I received my first pair of skis. My father, an avid skier, was still overseas; without him to instruct me, I just walked around on them in the snow. By the time I was six, I was going up the little rope tow at Whit's in Peterborough. The engine that powered the tow was a discarded motor from a retired Ford or Chevrolet. Whit had placed it in a shed at the bottom of the hill and attached it to a rope that, once grabbed, hauled skiers upward. Once, when I was six or seven, I skied down the little slope and, unable to stop, right into the shed and broke one of my skis. In tears I sought my father, who did not punish me as I feared, and, in fact, saw humor in the situation. By the next season, the shed with the engine was moved to the top of the hill.

In terms of sport, skiing was my father's passion, and his enthusiasm infected his children. During the war, he served with the 10th Mountain Division in Italy. When he returned, he brought with him two pairs of German skis and a pair of German ski boots, confiscated from the *Gerbisjager*, the German Mountain Division troops. Those white skis and brown ski boots became his trademark and lasted several seasons. I recall the embarrassment known so well to a pre-teen whose parent is non-conformist, watching my father lace up his boots and put on his skis in the early 1950s. How, we children wondered, could we make him get rid of them? Events dictated a solution. One morning, skiing down the Lift Line trail at Stowe, Vermont, Papa took a header. As he fell forward, his boot peeled from the sole. Once we saw that he was uninjured, we applauded the fall. New boots were purchased, followed shortly by new skis. Our embarrassment disappeared.

~

A wonderful annual event was the Children's Circus, conceived and masterminded by my older sister Mary and our cousin, Mary Fyffe, for the benefit of the Crotched Mountain Rehabilitation Center in Greenfield. The first circus was held in 1947 and was comprised of us children, a few cousins, and a small number of friends. The audience consisted of neighbors and parents who paid a nominal fee, along with a few children from the rehabilitation center. I forget what we raised that first year, but it was probably about $20, an amount that seemed enormous to us at the time. As the years went on, the Circus became larger and more elaborate. We assembled—horses, goats, clowns, floats and tumblers, dogs racing around and barking—and, under the organizational skills of the two Marys, paraded into the backyard before an audience seated on rented chairs. The 1957 Tenth Anniversary Program lists sixteen events, beginning with "The Grand Parade" and ending with "A Mad Brawl." Events included a "Dancer Divine" (Polly Hotchkiss, a cousin), "Equestriennes with Equilibrium" (with Betsy and Jenny and two friends), "Thousand-Legged Worm—Terrifying," and "Terrific, Tumultuous, Tumbling Tumble Weeds." Lemonade and cookies were sold to the guests. As the 1950s came to a close, so did the Circus; but memories persevered, as did lessons about giving. Mary continued to volunteer at the Rehabilitation Center. In the summer of 1959, newly graduated from high school, I recall visiting her there. A young boy, confined to a wheelchair, admired my new class ring and, because of lessons learned from my sister and cousin about caring and giving, I removed the ring and gave it to him.

∾

After the war, with my parents constantly producing more children (my father's older sister barraged them incessantly with information from Planned Parenthood, which my parents blithely tossed into the woodstove), the need for additional income became imperative. Commissions for pieces of sculpture ($75.00 for a bust of a child, involving two

Mary, Frank, and me, East River, Connecticut, c. 1944

months of work) and dividends from my father's skimpy portfolio did not cover the rising costs of increasing populations in both house and barn. Fortuitously, my parents' artistic leanings merged with practicality and, in 1947, they began to produce realistic toy animals made from rubber. The Gosling School, where I was a student, became their first customer. In 1950 the Educational Equipment Company—later to become Creative Playthings—became the largest customer.

By 1955 Red Shed Rubber Animals were sold in almost every state and in Alaska, Europe, the Middle East, Latin America, and Japan. Initially they were produced in my father's studio and in the kitchen. Soon the back porch was converted for production and eventually operations were moved to the upstairs of the Red Shed, located between the house and the barn.

∽

I remember the time my mother sliced off a piece of my ear as she was cutting my hair. I was about four and I remember looking at that bit of flesh lying forlornly on the floor. My mother, once realizing there was no real damage, found it amusing. I did not.

∽

There was another time on one of the rare Sundays when we attended the Unitarian Church. Squashed into two pews, we each had been given a nickel for the collection basket. Dutifully, though reluctantly, we parted with our coin and deposited it into the velvet-lined interior—until it came to George, who must have been two at the time. George, sensing that receiving was better than giving, reached in, grabbed a handful of money and promptly dropped it on the floor. At our parent's insistence, the rest of us scurried under the seats, retrieved the lost coins, and returned them to the basket still held by the patient, though stern-looking, usher. The minister labored bravely on.

∽

In 1948, my sister Mary and I had to walk just under a mile to catch the school bus. Once, loitering on the way (Mary had gone on ahead), I turned the corner just in time to see the rear of the bus disappear toward town. Elated, I skipped home with the prospect of a school-free day. My mother had other ideas. In a pique, and in silence, she drove me the four miles to school.

∽

We grew up with horses. We rode "English." Often, five or six of us would go out together. Trails through the woods and dirt roads allowed us to ride for miles, cantering or galloping down little-traveled paths, with Mitzi the Shetland—and the smartest and most cunning—out in front, cutting off those of us on larger horses, as we tried to pass her. We all took great pleasure in putting a "citified" visitor on Mitzi, because of her habit of taking her rider into a watering hole about half a mile from the barn; she then would kneel and begin to roll over.

We got a laugh, as the rider either quickly dismounted before being crushed, or risked getting very wet.

~

Summers, we would swim in Norway Pond in Hancock, taking time afterward to remove the two or three bloodsuckers (leeches) that clung to our bodies.

Winters, when we weren't skiing or doing chores, we often skated or played pick-up hockey on Fly Pond, about three miles back toward the village.

~

The hayloft was a wonderful place to play. I can still see the dust, highlighted in sun rays streaming down before the big door, and can smell the mustiness of hay, heightened by aromas from the barn below. Once, Frank, my cousin Sandy Greene, and I built a trap by placing loose hay over an open trap door in the floor that was typically used to toss hay to the horses and goats below. Our intent was to lure my sister Mary and Sandy's older sister, BAnne, across the floor and over the disguised opening. Frank and I were standing as lookouts for the girls. When one of us called, "Here they come!" Sandy dashed toward us and crashed through the trap he had helped lay. I turned just in time to see the top of his head as he, with a cry, disappeared to the floor below. Other than his pride, Sandy was unhurt, and Frank and I had a story to tell.

~

Growing up in the late 1940s and early 1950s meant coming of age in the wake of World War II and under the cloud of the atomic bomb. Memorial Day had tremendous meaning in those years. Most of the veterans who marched in the annual parade had seen recent service. There were older veterans, in their late forties and early fifties, who had fought in World War I, and even a few old-timers who had served during the Spanish-American War. The horrors of the conflicts were very much alive, not only for those who had been in combat, but also for the families of the seventeen from Peterborough who died in the two World Wars. Frank and I would ride our bikes four miles to the village and, joined by several others, follow the parade to Pine Hill Cemetery. On the bridge that crossed the Contoocook, in front of the library, a wreath would be tossed to the waters below and we would watch as the current carried it away, north toward the Merrimac and thence south to the sea. Later at the cemetery, where my parents and paternal grandparents now lie, Taps was played, its somber notes echoing back on the breeze. We were largely spared the scare of nuclear holocaust (other than the occasional, and futile, dive under a desk in school during a drill) by a family and a village that concentrated on the present and, while neither ignorant nor unaware of the risks in international brinkmanship, placed it in a context befitting young and impressionable children. There would be time enough to confront the monster of reality. This was a time to be young.

$\sim$

Reliving these stories, I am reminded of the lines from Kenneth Grahame's *The Wind in the Willows*: "The Mole was bewitched, entranced, fascinated. By the side of the river he trotted as one trots, when very small, by the side of a man who holds one spell-bound by exciting stories; and when tired at last, he sat on the bank, while the river still chattered on to him, a babbling procession of the best stories in the world, sent from the heart of the earth to be told at last to the insatiable sea." Stories from our past are the best stories. They allow readers to consume a slice of history. For my children and grandchildren, I hope they provide an opportunity to learn something of their heritage, along with the prospect of a better understanding of themselves.

The Death of My Father, Some Forty Years On

Forty years on, when afar and asunder
Parted are those who are singing today,
When you look back, and forgetfully wonder
What you were like in your work and your play,
Then, it may be, there will often come o'er you,
Glimpses of notes like the catch of a song—
Visions of boyhood shall float them before you,
Echoes of dreamland shall bear them along.

Words from the song, "Forty Years On"
Edward Ernest Brown and John Farmer, 1872

SITTING AT THE DINING ROOM TABLE is where I remember him best. In my mind's eye, my brother Frank is usually there, and we are between ten and fourteen. Dishes have been cleared. One of us is generally sitting atop the woodstove, which heated the dining room and the living room, the warmest spot in the house on cold winter days. It is our conversations that stay with me. My brother and I would argue with our father, in a Socratic manner with adolescent fervor, searching for explanations and answers. Papa, pipe always at hand, would respond calmly and with humor, a well-thumbed dictionary within easy reach. It was the way we learned. He supplemented his arguments with stories from fiction and his childhood and we learned colorful stories from our family's past. Once I left for school, college, marriage, and then work, the scene was no doubt repeated, as my younger siblings submitted themselves to this didactic process.

My father died on December 2, 1968, at far too young an age. He had been a smoker his entire life, giving up cigarettes only a few years before his death. The cancer that began in his lungs metastasized to his brain where it first manifested itself. A glass dropped on the kitchen floor was the first inkling that all was not well. He died ten months later.

As I was twenty-seven when he died, I was one of the fortunate ones.

My youngest sibling, George, was only thirteen and so missed much of the wisdom and comfort Papa offered to me as a boy and as a young father.

He grew up in circumstances very different from the life he lived, as I knew him, on a small, rocky farm in New Hampshire. There he lived the life of an impecunious artist, and raised, with my mother, the nine children to whom he referred in a twenty-fifth college reunion note as his "nine ideas."

But he had been brought up in Wellesley, Massachusetts, in the house

My father, c. 1914

in which his mother had been born in 1875. Her grandfather had been a merchant banker in Paris, who returned to Boston around 1850 and became a successful investor in the newly industrialized United States. My great-great-grandfather had enormous love for his expanding family, and built homes and beautiful gardens on abutting properties for his children. It was one of those houses, a classic Victorian, that was home to my father throughout his childhood and until he was married. His parents also owned a summer place—a farm on several hundred acres—in Peterborough. It was there that my father's love and imagination were truly captivated. During vacations, friends from the Belmont Hill School, and later Harvard, would come to visit. And on the property was the small house that became my parents home when they married in the late spring of 1938.

My father was consumed by nightmares as a child, and twice affected by serious illness, once in childhood and again as a teen. It is not unreasonable to assume that those latter experiences—which involved hospitalization and long stretches in bed—may have later fueled his interest in physical fitness. While a freshman in college, he took up row-

My father, with his parents, c. 1934

ing although his height and stature kept him from being competitive. But hiking and, especially, skiing became activities he pursued all his life. In the summer of 1929, he spent two or three months bicycling through England, Scotland, and France with one of his close friends, John Farlow. John later recounted a time during college when they decided to hike Skatudakee Mountain in Hancock over Washington's Birthday weekend, in the midst of a snowstorm. He and my father "took turns breaking trail on the road. It was about six miles north and six miles back, and if I'm not making light of the situation, it was two below zero in Peterborough. When we got to the top, the wind was so strong we had to go on hands and knees. And by that time it was fifteen below zero." They made it back safely, but the effort clearly demanded grit and determination. My father was apparently so exhausted that he wanted to sit down and sleep, but his friend helped him keep pushing onward and reported afterward, "We had a good trip."

Papa finished college in June of 1932 but, according to my grandmother, was unhappy with his thesis and did not get his degree. By that time the Depression had taken strong hold of the country and jobs were

Papa milking Mocha, c. 1946

hard to come by. He tried his hand at cartooning—something he had first dabbled in at college—but was unable to sell any drawings to the Boston papers. He worked for a while as a receptionist, carving pipes to while away time, until one day he simply decided not to go back. He began to volunteer at Harvard College, modeling bugs in the Entomology Department. He also did some modeling of the backgrounds for display cases at the Fogg Museum. At some point, probably in 1935 or 1936, a family friend looked at his work and suggested he study sculpture. Thus, in 1937 he found himself in Gloucester, Massachusetts, learning to cut stone at the studio of George Demetrios.

It was in Gloucester that he met my mother. My father was never noted as a lady's man, and certainly he was something of a loner. He always seemed happiest in the natural world and with his art. In my mother he found a symbiotic partner. They shared a devotion to art, and particularly to sculpture. Her interest in horses matched his interest in skiing. She was the practical one; he the more whimsical. Shortly before their marriage he ended a letter to her saying, "Give my regards to anybody that might like them. Don't waste them on people who wouldn't care, but give them to any birds and flowers that you see or any animals or anything beautiful and to everything that likes you."

Once married and living in Peterborough, my parents' life was incredibly simple. My father had a small income (perhaps $2,500 a year); my mother had none. Art was a difficult sale during this time, and children began arriving, so, eventually my father decided he needed anoth-

Papa on skis, c. 1954, Stuart in background

er source of income. He had no interest in putting on a suit; he wanted a simple, self-sufficient life. Margaret Perry, an old friend of his parents, offered him regular farm work and he accepted, commuting six miles each way every day by horse and carriage.

But the war was raging in Europe; eventually even men like my father—in his thirties and with small children—were needed. In April 1944, when I was three and shortly before my sister Betsy was born, my father was drafted into the army. Along with about 9,500 other men, he endured nine days of a stormy Atlantic crossing on the U.S.S. West Point, finally docking in Naples, Italy, on January 13, 1945. In a letter to my mother, he described the trip: "The boat trip wasn't too bad, though even a sardine would have called it cozy. I'd breathe once morning and evening and not bother the rest of the day." He served with the 10th Mountain Division, winning a Bronze Star for meritorious service in combat in the Italian Apennines. Although he was slated to join the planned invasion of Japan in the fall,

Papa in his studio, c. 1950

by August the Japanese had surrendered, and by November he came home for good.

Both my parents were artists, and so my father's days were spent at home. He would get up early, light the woodstove, put on the oatmeal, check the coal-fired hot water furnace, and head to the barn. At some point in the mid 1950s, my mother, never much for housekeeping, assumed the barn chores, but in the early post-war years that was Papa's province. Early morning involved feeding and milking the goats, feeding the chickens, gathering any eggs, and feeding and putting the horses out to pasture. The barn was built of weather-beaten, unpainted boards. It was large, with pens for the goats, a chicken coop, and horse stalls. It had a hayloft above and a manure pit below and exuded an odorous, but warm and comfortable feeling.

My father was a life-long Republican, and he disliked President Franklin Roosevelt. I recall, once, coming home from school—a young wise-assed kid—going to the barn where my father was in the midst of milking some unfortunate goat. My teacher had read to us of Roosevelt and the packing of the Supreme Court. I suggested to my father that it sounded like a sensible move, given the problem his administration was having at that time with the courts. The goat bleated and jumped about, the innocent victim of my father's anger, as he yanked her teats impulsively.

He was, otherwise, a genial man. He had a slight build—about my size—standing about five-foot-nine. He was lean and muscular and proud of his strength and of his physical well being—not from working out, but from constant physical labor. His normal attire was blue jeans, with a blue work shirt in the summer and a green-and-black plaid woolen shirt in colder weather. I never remember seeing him in shorts or polo-type shirts. His hands were calloused, as he rarely wore gloves, and his hair, graying at the temples, was cut short by my mother. He was quiet, shy, and polite in an old-fashioned way. My wife recalls him standing when she first met him. He had a good sense of humor, but never liked ethnic and off-color jokes; his sense of humor was disarming, creative, and gentle. Other than when he was in the service during the war, he rarely wrote letters and he was never comfortable on the telephone. Not being able to see the person to whom he was speaking made conversation difficult for him. I remember long silences, periodically interrupted by a harrumph and a puff on his pipe.

He had little respect for convention, and so had no trouble taking us out of school to ski if a big snowstorm blew through. Of course, as an artist, it made little difference to him whether he worked on Tuesday or on Sunday. We might, on a week day, jump into the car and drive to Sunapee, leaving my mother at home to care for the younger children and deal with the animals.

Papa loved to ski and to ski fast, standing straight on his captured German skis and wearing his captured German ski boots, brought home from Italy. While he never wore the insignia of the 10th Mountain Division after the war, we often ran into other veterans and he always spoke to them. He gave in to his children more than he should have. Once, in Stowe, we had the opportunity to hear the von Trapp Family Singers. He let us put the decision to a vote and we chose to see a movie instead. He should have overridden us, but he didn't.

Papa with busts of me, Frank, and Mary

Every Christmas Eve brought an expedition—a trip into the woods to cut down a tree. Papa would hitch Judy to a sledge and off we would go—never very far, perhaps a half-mile at the most—to bring home a fresh tree that he decorated with real candles. That evening, before the annual reading of *The Night before Christmas*, he would bring Mitzi, our Shetland pony, into the house as we hung our stockings, so that she could hang her "shoe" over the fireplace. During the night Santa would leave an apple tied to it and, in the morning, Mitzi would return to the living room, my father beside her, to accept the gift.

Vignettes of him stay in my mind—outside on a spring day chopping wood, his shirt off; mowing the grass on a summer afternoon with the quiet clicking of the hand mower; gathering leaves, in late autumn, to press against the house's foundation as a means to provide natural (but insufficient) insulation; replacing steel edges at the end of a winter's day of skiing. Hundreds of these visions remain in my mind, available for instant recall; the passage of time has neither diminished their number nor faded them.

After my maternal grandfather died in 1947, my grandmother exhorted me to remember him often, "For when you do," she said, "he will come alive." It took me a few years to realize the wisdom of that simple advice. She was right. People do come alive when we recall them, if only in our own memories, but that is sufficient. More than forty years on I still miss my father and think of him often; Robert Service's lines from his poem, *The Spell of the Yukon*, come to mind, "It's the beauty that thrills with words, / It's the stillness that fills with peace." I feel better.

My Mother—Some Vignettes

I conceived a memorial to Youth–a plunging horse, riderless, nostrils quivering, his mane and tail on fire, and every muscle taut, but collected; free from silken reins of convention, just the symbolic spirit of dynamic youth, unguided and confident.

Letter from my mother, Mary B. W. Hotchkiss,
Winter, 1936, Influenced by the death of King George V

D ESPITE HAVING NINE CHILDREN TO RAISE, horses always came first in my mother's life. Art, especially sculpture, was not far behind; however, her interest in sculpting gradually gave way to the demands of family and everyday life . . . and horses. She grew up in her grandfather's house in New Haven, Connecticut, behind which was a stable. Her grandfather had a coachman, Taylor, who had been born a slave. Horses were the only world Taylor knew. My mother spent hours in the stable where he infused in her a love for the animal—a love that lasted the rest of her life. In 1974, she wrote a letter to her children and grandchildren entitled "Horses, and What They Have Meant to Me." In that letter she wrote, "The day I was married I got up at daybreak and went for a long ride alone with Charmer and my dogs Peter and his son Brutus.[2] The day after Papa [my father] died, though it was December, I saddled Star and rode to the top of the hill alone. There, the storm clouds that bleak December morning suddenly opened up, and the rising sun lit the edges of the black clouds. I patted Star, and knew I could make it." She did. Mama died twenty-two years after my father, on the same date (December 2).

~

---

2 She carved a tombstone for Brutus when he died in 1941, which now rests in our garden in Old Lyme. For me, that marble slab is a link to the past, and provides a sense of the continuum of life.

"Cottage on beach"—so reads the location on the paper certifying Mama's birth in East River, Connecticut, on July 21, 1911. That location was repeated by my mother three or four times in a wonderful interview conducted by a former sister-in-law, Sue Martin, about a year before my mother died in 1990. She said "reviewing my life is like reading somebody else's biography, to think about my childhood and how I was brought up." East River, in the southwestern section of Madison, is where she spent many happy days of her youth. My grandfather had bought about forty acres, including a cottage on Long Island Sound around 1910. In 1918, the cottage was torn down and a larger house was built, which he named "Wyndham," my grandmother's middle name. Holidays, weekends, and summers were spent there. My mother kept her horses in a barn my grandfather had built. Early on, almost all the roads in the area were dirt (including the Boston Post Road). They became the venue of choice for my mother and her friends, as they rode their horses for miles. In the 1974 letter to her children, she wrote about her first horse, Tippy, given to her when she was eight. "She shared my moods, gave me mobility and taught me self-reliance and independence."

It was from Tippy that my mother also learned that actions have consequences. "One fall night," she wrote, "Tippy died of pneumonia. My world shattered. I had been swimming her in Long Island Sound . . . . It was my fault and it took a long time before I could even mention her name."

In the winters, the family lived in New Haven with her grandfather in a large house at the top of Hillhouse Avenue. The Italianate brownstone is still there and now belongs to Yale University. My great-grandfather bought it in 1888, later adding a wing that doubled its size. He lived there with my grandfather and grandmother, my great-grandmother having died in 1902. When my grandmother arrived from Tennessee in 1907 as a bride of eighteen, she took charge of a large staff led by a Scottish butler, Dallas, who my mother described as being "good to us even though we were mean to him."

Another household figure that my mother always remembered was

My mother off to dancing class, Taylor at the reins, c. 1923

Pit, an Englishwoman who had helped raise her mother in Tennessee and in Washington, D.C. Pit had come to New Haven when my grandmother married and remained with her until she died. Pit apparently was later a fierce defender of my mother and her siblings (an older brother and two younger ones) whenever the need arose, which happened with some frequency, for the children were noted for misdemeanors like firing BB guns at passing horses and bicyclists.

The third member of the staff that my mother remembered with great fondness was the aforementioned Taylor. Every couple of days Taylor would exercise the horses. When she was about ten, my mother convinced her grandfather that the seven-mile trip from their home to the Hamden Hall School, where dancing lessons were conducted, would be the perfect distance for exercising horses; so that is how she would arrive—wearing a white pinafore, seated in her grandfather's carriage, driven by a man who had been born a slave. I have a photo of her sitting in the carriage in front of 55 Hillhouse; she is wearing her white pinafore and a white hat; Taylor is sitting erect, whip in hand; the two horses look alert. Perhaps she is off to dancing lessons? It seems so incongruous to me today, for in truth she hated dresses, both as a child and as an adult. My mother was always more tomboy than a child who played with dolls.

My mother, c. 1930

Her grandfather, my great-grandfather, died in 1930, and the house in New Haven was sold shortly afterward, its sale hastened by the fact that my mother's father had invested heavily with Ivar Krueger, best known as the Swedish Match king and whose financial fraud was only surpassed by that of Bernie Madoff in 2008.

~

As a child and young woman, my mother was creative. She wrote light and amusing poetry. The last few lines of "Lauretta, a Race Horse," written when she was about nine, read:

> *The home stretch now, before the eyes of the noble*
> *Horses lay.*
>
> *She passed the Queen, and took first place, and*
> *There she planned to stay.*
>
> *Lauretta entered the stable as proud as a horse*
> *Could be.*
>
> *For she kicked the Queen to kingdom come*
> *And that was the cause of her glee.*

I have a half-dozen, framed Christmas cards my mother designed and sent out, a custom that continued into her early married years. They are pen and ink—usually black and red—simple line drawings with a modern and elegant simplicity. Most, but not all, include horses. Hanging on a wall in our mudroom is a double-framed combination poem and drawing she did in 1941, entitled "Ode to October," the birth and wedding month of her parents. It begins and concludes with the refrain:

> October is a happy month,
> A month of love and song,
> Of being wed and giving birth
> And dancing all day long!

In 1936 at the age of 25, she privately printed a short poem that she had written and illustrated, entitled "Muldoon Mouse":

> On the bottom step of our house
> There lives the most wonderful mouse
>
> He isn't at all like his aunt,
> She swishes her tail, and he can't.

A year earlier, she had been in competition to illustrate a novel, *Young Entry*, for the author Gordon Grand. The editors of Derrydale Press selected the (then) well-known illustrator of sporting books, Paul Brown. But Gordon Grand had brought my mother's illustrations in for consideration. In 1936, while teaching at the Foxcroft School in Virginia, she ended the letter quoted at the start of this essay: "So I shall go on, firm in the belief that Nature, the art of God, consciously or unconsciously must be the keystone to the art of man."

∼

With her mother and two youngest brothers, she took a trip in early 1924 through the Panama Canal. They sailed from New York on the S.S.

My mother's engagement photo, 1937

Kroonland, then owned by the Panama Pacific Line. While her brothers were (or became) sailors, my mother's interest in horses kept her a "land lubber." She wrote to her grandfather in early January: "Passing Cape Hatteras it was quite rough and I felt a little queer, as though I would give a million dollars to be on land again." But, at the same time *her* mother writes her father-in-law: "We have had a marvelous passage! Hardly a bit of motion, even off Hatteras." I have a framed memento of that trip. Among the passengers was the creator of the comic strip "Reg'lar Fellers," the cartoonist Gene Byrne. It is a cartoon of two of his "Fellers," one saying to the other, "Don't say nothin' if I tell ya! I got a SWELL new goil named MARY HOTCHKISS!"

In the fall of 1926 Mama went to the Foxcroft School in Middleburg, Virginia, a place she came to love. The school was founded by Miss Charlotte Noland in 1914. Miss Charlotte, as she was known, was still there when my sister entered the school in 1954. Foxcroft is close to Washington, where my grandmother had lived for several years, but, more important to my mother, she could bring her horse as Middleburg is in the middle of Virginia hunt country. Besides riding, she played field hockey, and basketball, and was generally popular. She returned to the school in 1934 to teach art.

Instead of college, after graduating from Foxcroft she enrolled (along with a Foxcroft classmate) in Madame Boni's school in Rome. Despite living in Rome and being married to an Italian, Madame Boni was French. The seven girls at the school—four Americans, two English girls, and one from Scotland—were expected to speak French at all times. Madame Boni's was, in the vernacular of the day, a finishing school.

Mama also spent a year in Sweden, traveling with my grandfather when he was asked by the Irving Trust Company to represent their interests in the Ivar Kreuger financial debacle. For my mother, at the age of twenty-one and unencumbered by worldly worries, the trip was a wonderful opportunity to return to Europe, to travel, to ride, and to study art. And as Kreuger had been a close friend of Greta Garbo, my mother and grandfather were able to live in her apartment during the time they were in Sweden.

~

It was art that brought my parents together. In the summer of 1936, they both happened to study sculpture in the studio of George Demetrios in Gloucester, Massachusetts. My mother's first cousin, Mary Blagden, had studied under Mr. Demetrios the previous fall in Philadelphia; the plan was that both Marys would go to Massachusetts. Mama's cousin, however, went off to Europe, so my mother went alone. The group of students was small, about eight all together, but included my father, Sydney. Mama spent that summer in Gloucester and then, along with my father and some of the other students, went to Boston where Mr. Demetrios taught during the winter. The summer of 1937 saw them back in Gloucester. Sometime that summer my parents realized they were in love. In a letter Mama wrote to her mother, she tells her that Sydney proposed. She writes, "…unless you have any good or strong objection I'm beginning to realize it [my answer] will be 'yes.'" Their engagement was announced on September 26, 1937.

They were married on May 28, 1938, at Center Church in New Haven. It was in the midst of the Depression, and my grandfather, unbeknownst to his family, had gone into debt to maintain his lifestyle. The reception was held at "Wyndham," their home in East River. Unusual for the time, my mother's five bridesmaids and matron of honor came from six different states, including Texas and California. After a short honeymoon, my parents moved into the house in Peterborough where they would live for the next thirty years, interrupted only when my mother returned briefly to Connecticut while my father was overseas in the war.

The house in New Hampshire was far different from what Mama had been used to. It had plumbing but no electricity, and was heated by a woodstove. It was four miles from the village and, at the time, at the end of a dirt road. (I have often wondered about my grandmother's reaction when she first came to visit!)

But it was a perfect place for struggling young artists who had chosen to isolate themselves from a world that appeared to be going mad. It was a place to forget the Depression, which was in its ninth year, and to hide from the clouds of war gathering ominously over Europe. They concentrated on sculpture. Most of the pieces Mama made were of horses, modeled in clay; she would then create a plaster mold from which emerged the finished product in Plaster-of-Paris. After Mama died, my brother Stuart encouraged the copying of her many pieces in bronze. One of her pieces, "South Wind," a horse nuzzling her foal, was given in her memory to the Kentucky Horse Park in Lexington, Kentucky, and now sits in the Grand Prix Seminar Room. (My youngest brother, George, is a member of the U.S. Equestrian Team and has represented the United States in international competition, winning fifth place at the 2003 World Cup in Sweden.)

Children started arriving: my sister Mary in April 1939, and then me in January 1941. By the time my brother Frank was born, the U.S. was engulfed in a world war. My father, a thirty-three-year-old father of three, was drafted into the Army in the early spring of 1944. That August, before my father was shipped to Italy, another child, Betsy, was born.

～

After the war it soon became apparent that sculpting and my father's small income would be insufficient to support the number of children they intended to raise: Charlotte was born in July 1946; Jenny in 1948; Stuart in 1950; Willard in the spring of 1952, and George in September 1955. The decision to produce toy animals was serendipitous. My mother, as a sculptor and lover of animals, was surrounded by cats, dogs,

My mother, May 28, 1938

My mother in her studio, c. 1950

chickens, ducks, goats, horses, and, later, peacocks. She wanted toy animals for her children that would be realistic, yet durable. Her father,
having spent much of his career in the rubber business, urged my parents to use rubber as a medium.

Working in clay and then creating a rubber animal from a mold
proved inexpensive and productive. The first toy animals were made in
our kitchen using the oven in the woodstove to "bake" the molds. The
first rubber animals accompanied me to kindergarten at the Gosling
School in 1947. The first ones to bring a profit were sold through the
New Hampshire League of Arts and Crafts. Within a year, they came
to the attention of a man named Murray Shapiro who ran Educational
Equipment Company of New York, which partnered with Bank Street
College in New York City (from which my daughter Linie later received
a Master's degree) to supply the Bank Street Nursery School. By 1949,
4,200 pieces were being produced for the school.

My mother always kept the right perspective regarding the business.
In her personally typed 1955 annual report, "Mama and Papa Williams"

are shown as the owners, with the nine of us children listed as shareholders. Liabilities included "no trip to Stowe" and "Papa's worn out suit." Assets included a "new shareholder" (George, who is pictured on the cover) and a "pony cart." My mother expressed dismay at the lack of investment made by the shareholders. The report instructed the shareholders that the way to receive "larger dividends" was through "investments," by which Mama meant "dishwashing," "barn cleaning," "house sweeping," and "baby tending." "All of these investments are encouraged for the sole purpose of allowing the owners to invest their time in increasing the profits for all concerned, both monetary and pleasurable." In conclusion she wrote, "The demand continues. The future looks good. Now is the time to increase your investments in this growing business and write this year's liabilities in next year's asset sheet."

Operations moved to the second floor of a large red shed that stood between our house and barn, and three women were hired to trim and paint the figures. My mother designed and made the clay figures; my father produced the rubber molds using a process he developed. By the mid 1950s, seventy-five different figures were being produced—puppets, hobby horses, farm and domestic toy animals, a series of wild animals and the people figures to accompany them. By that time they were being sold in every state, plus Alaska (which was not yet a state.) They were sold in Europe, Japan, and the Middle East as well. My mother took special pride in a television appeal by Helen Keller for funds for blind children that showed children playing with Red Shed Rubber Animals.

In January 1969, a month after my father had died, my mother was interviewed in *Family Circle*. She said: "We could have started a factory operation. But we believed in our way of life—the kind of life that made it possible for my husband to be a sculptor. We are artists, not industrialists." After he died, the rubber animal business gradually faded away; my mother returned to what she loved best, horses and the teaching of riding. However, the product survives and my grandchildren today play with rubber animals created in that red shed so long ago.

~

When my father died at the age of fifty-eight on December 2, 1968, he left my mother, age fifty-seven, with sole responsibility for caring for the three children still at home: Stuart, age eighteen; Willard, age 16; and George, age 13. The four oldest of us were married and starting families. Charlotte, age 22, would be married the following spring and Jenny, age 20, was at college. My mother was instrumental in the ultimate success of the three youngest children. George became a member of the U.S. Equestrian Team. Willard founded and is the owner-operator of The Toadstool Bookshop, one of New England's pre-eminent independent bookstores. Stuart became a successful artist. He has exhibited in New Hampshire, Boston, and New York, and his work is on display at the Currier Museum of Art in Manchester, New Hampshire. As the years went on, Stuart remained my mother's constant companion. She once told him that she could not have survived without him. He kept her company when loneliness threatened.

~

We held a seventy-fifth birthday party for my mother at my sister Mary's home in Henniker, New Hampshire, in July of 1986. All of her children and grandchildren were there. She composed a poem (with apologies to Lewis Carroll) to mark the occasion:

> "You look old Granny Williams," the young ones all cried.
> "And your hair has become very white,
> But still you insist you'llcontinue to ride.
> Do you think at your age it is right?"
>
> "Yes I do and I will," Granny Williams confessed.
> "'Til the judge up above rings the bell,
> Then I'll enter at 'A' and ride my Last test.
> And I'll pray that I will really do well."

Mama on "Dude," 1979

I'll halt squarely at 'X' and heave a great sigh,
Since my hair has become very white,
Tip my hat to the judge, then I'll bid him goodbye,
And I'll slowly fade out of sight."

But not yet; never fear, I'll continue to ride,
Though my hair has become very white.
I'll just climb on my horse and I'll flow with the tide.
For I think at my age it is right."

She continued to teach riding and to ride herself, though her knees, which had long been a problem, made walking difficult. In fact, the morning of the day she died she gave a lesson.

～

My mother was far from perfect. As children, we soon learned that our place came behind that of her favorite animals. Her admonishing letters, when we were away at school, could be hard to take; though, in retrospect, her advice was generally appropriate. Diplomacy was not

[65]

A few days before her death on December 2, 1990

her strong suit. If she did not like someone, she had difficulty hiding her feelings. She was more sympathetic than empathetic. But she was unique. Mama was talented, as an artist and horsewoman, and she had a mind of her own. She was, as one of her nephews once said, guided by her own star. Not once did I ever hear her utter a harsh word about her father whom she loved deeply, despite his financial reversals. The evening Mitzi, our Shetland pony, died in the early 1960s, Mama was in the barn, Mitzi's head cradled on her lap, as she breathed her last. My mother taught hundreds of young people, not only how to ride, but how to love and care for horses. And she successfully raised nine children, all of whom have done well in their individual ways.

The last time I saw her was an evening in Peterborough and all of her children were there except George. She wasn't that old—seventy-nine—but she seemed tired, yet also quietly content. My wife Caroline noticed, and spoke to her as we were leaving, telling her she had never seen her looking so much at peace. Mama died in her sleep less than thirty hours later.

We are all placed on earth for a relatively short time. People leave their mark in various ways, some through gifts of great art and architecture, others through philanthropies and literature, and others simply through the gift of life they provide their descendants. My mother traveled a great distance, some would say from "riches to rags," but she would disagree (as do I). Her legacy left the world a richer place for her presence. Early on, she recognized that life is a gift. Some people let events control their destiny. Others, like my mother, seize life and make it work for them. The events that cost her father his fortune were beyond her control; she never let setbacks deter her pursuit of the life she chose—horses, art, and family.

The memory of my mother is etched in the minds of all who knew her, including her many students. Her love of horses is reflected in my brother George's chosen career as a dressage rider of international repute. It is reflected in my two sisters, Betsy and Jenny, who have lived with horses since they left home, teaching new generations the love of riding. Her love for art is mirrored in Stuart's creations, and her pieces sit in the homes of her children and grandchildren, as well as in the horse museum in Lexington. Her many heirs—her more than sixty children, grandchildren, and great-grandchildren, those who inherited her genes—will forever keep her spirit alive.

"Granny" Hotchkiss and Mary Washington Williams, c. 1940

Charlotte is 4th from left; Betsy & Jenny are 3rd and 2nd from right, September 22, 1962

Eulogy for My Sister, Mary Williams Gregg

Delivered at the Unitarian Church, Peterborough, New Hampshire,
December 8, 1997

MARY WAS THE MOTHER OF US ALL. Obviously, I don't mean that in a literal sense. Mary and Bebo's devoted children would take exception. But I think most of you know what I mean. We all looked to Mary as the perfect mother—devoted, caring, attentive. We all felt somewhat submissive in her presence. Perhaps it was her use of signs—signs everywhere:

> Latch the door.
> Wipe your feet.
> Take off your shoes.
> *No* boots upstairs.
> Close the damper.

Maybe it was her organizational skills:

> Weekends fully planned.
> Coats, hats, gloves—all in their respective places.
> The kitchen table set for breakfast before she went to bed.

But in my case, and those of my siblings, this mothering went back further—much further. When I was born, my parents saw in me their first son, but Mary saw a new plaything!

In my memory, it is an afternoon during the War. Mary and I are in our grandparent's house in Madison, Connecticut. I am standing on a bed trying on a skirt, or, rather, Mary is trying the skirt on me. On my feet is a pair of shiny, black "Mary Janes."

Another memory—it is a year or two later and we are in Peterborough. It is a pleasant, late spring day, a day for playing outside. My brother Frank is with me. I am perhaps five and Frank three. We are sitting in front of the lilacs—behind a pair of desks! Mary towers over

Papa with Mary in Peterborough, c. 1941

us, commanding a blend of fear and respect. She is determined that we learn our letters, letters that Mary most likely learned at school that morning. These experiences with Mary were not unique. I share them with all my siblings. I also share them with many of you. I simply was the oldest and thus the first to be subjected to Mary's mothering, yet instructional, ways.

As I got older, her nurturing never diminished. She had advice about the girls I dated, at times pleasant and encouraging, at others disparaging. So, when Mary introduced me to the woman who would become my wife, I was both happy and relieved. As the years went by she continued dispensing advice and counsel. I will miss it. And so, I know, will all of you.

Mary's mothering showed in her devotion to all children, but especially to her own—Mary, Robin, Bobby, and Walter. When they were young, she was like the proverbial mother hen, letting them out to play, ensuring they ate, and then, come evening, shepherding them back into the security of her home. To measure her success, all you have to do is meet her children. Mary's love for children extended to her twenty nieces and nephews, all of whom are here today and six of whom are ushering.

Papa and Mama with Mary in East River, c. 1940

Early on, Mary's devotion manifested itself in her role as founder, director, and stage manager of the Children's Circus. Mary started the Children's Circus at our home in Peterborough in 1947. She was eight years old and already a take-charge individual. It was, at the start, a reason to create, organize, and execute an event—a "happening," as we would say today. We lived on a small farm, with horses, goats, and chickens, and by 1947, five children. Additionally, there were cousins, friends, and neighbors. This all provided plenty of material with which Mary could work. The Circus became an outstanding success. Every August, people from all over the area, including many of you, would descend on the Dodge farm (as our place was called). The Circus provided Mary an opportunity to show a new side of her character—her devotion to charity and her empathy for those less fortunate. In the first years, the proceeds were minimal, but in 1953 Harry Gregg, the father of former governor Hugh Gregg, established the Crotched Mountain Rehabilitation Center. In its early years, the Center was largely devoted to children with polio and cerebral palsy. From that time on, the Center became the beneficiary of all proceeds raised. Each annual Circus earned a column in the *Peterborough Transcript*. The tents were finally struck in 1958. Mary was nineteen. She was at college; her interests had turned elsewhere.

Yet her devotion to children and charity persisted. Barely had the last memories of the Circus dissipated when she began volunteering at Ellis Memorial in Boston. Her donations of time and energy continued through years of dedicated service to schools in Henniker, New Hampshire; to Agawam, a boy's camp in Maine; and to teaching skiing at Pat's Peak.

Another dimension of Mary worth noting was her physical, mental, and spiritual toughness. Mary lived life to the hilt. Every moment was full. Her motto could easily have been "*carpe diem.*" To her, it wasn't the distance of the race or even where you finished, but how well did you run and did you give it your best. Mary was one of those people that never had to say, "if only. . . ."

Mary, as most of you know, never worked for anyone other than herself. That created an indomitable belief in herself. She did not belong to any organized church, but there was no doubt she was a spiritual person. Despite periodic obstacles, she was persistently cheerful. Nothing, not even the cancer that began to riddle her body, could keep her spirits down. I recall one day, less than two years ago, in February of 1996. It was a family ski day at Mount Sunapee. Mary was there with two of her children, Robin and Walter, if memory serves. My three other sisters, Betsy, Charlotte, and Jenny were along, and so was my brother Willard. The snow conditions were hard and fast. The day was overcast and foggy. Cancer had already spread to Mary's bone structure. We were heading home—the last run off the top of the mountain, coming down the Hansen Chase trail. Robin, Walter, and Betsy had gone ahead. Charlotte and Jenny disappeared into the mist. I cannot recall where Willard was. We were traveling fast, as Williams' are wont to do on skis. Suddenly, I heard the clatter of skis to my right. It was Mary. She scooted on by. About two hundred yards ahead was an old logging road that crossed the trail. The effect of crossing such a path, if you do not cross it at an angle, is a jump. Mary headed straight for the path—and the jump. I swore. Mary soared 40 or 50 feet through the air, landed upright and disappeared into the fog. When I reached the bottom, Mary turned,

Mary and Robert "Bebo" Gregg, September 22, 1962

still slightly breathless and her eyes bright: "Did you see how much air I got?" That was Mary.

It was that same tenacity and daring that kept Mary alive for so long, and made it difficult for her to accept death. Her daughter Robin said to me a few weeks ago that it was her will that kept her alive. Robin was right. It was her will—her grit. The fight Mary put up makes Steven Vincent Benet's story of the Devil and Daniel Webster seem like a welter-weight competition in comparison. Given the outcome, we can only conclude God really wanted her.

Mary with daughters Mary, on her right, and Robin, on her left

Over the weekend of November 9, Mary and Bebo took a last trip through Vermont and New York State, culminating at "Briar Patch," their camp in the Adirondacks. Mary, speaking later to me about the trip, said she had commented to Bebo on the bleakness of the day—the trees, leafless; the sky, overcast. Bebo then suggested that the beauty, at this time of year, was that you could look into the woods and see the individual trees. You could see houses that otherwise were hidden. And so Mary, as we sat with her those last few days before she slipped into a coma, seemed to be looking at each of us—absent any foliage, into our very souls. Those were the portraits she wanted to accompany her on her long voyage.

So, Mary, because of you and your signs, your caring, and your love, when we, too, make our exits, we will remember to check the furnace, turn out the lights, and lock the door behind us. God bless you, Mary. We love you.

Stuart Hotchkiss Williams
December 2, 1950–May 15, 2012

Each handicap is like a hurdle in a steeplechase and when you ride up to it,
if you throw your heart over, the horse will go along too.

Lawrence Bixby (1895–1982)
Cattle Rancher

M Y BROTHER STUART WAS FOREMOST AN ARTIST. He was largely self-taught, although he did study at the Sharon Arts Center in New Hampshire for two years. He had an eye for color and an appreciation of animals and nature. He had humor that manifested itself in the titles of many of his pieces, and in the way in which an animal might peer out from within a bush or from behind their mother. Despite his formidable handicaps and a dark world caused by frustration that at times enveloped his mind, it is the presence of a yellow sun that we notice on many, if not most, of his canvasses. Stuart was well aware of how he was different from others, and there were times when those demons dominated, but his paintings display a far sunnier and optimistic view.

My brother was born with a rare genetic disorder that was undiagnosed at the time of his birth. Six years later, two physicians, Andrea Prader and Heinrich Willi, identified and described the symptom that came to be known as Prader-Willi Syndrome (PWS). The classic signs of PWS are a constant craving for food and a rapid gain in weight. It manifests itself in short stature, obesity, small hands and feet, low muscle mass, delayed puberty, speech problems, and mild to moderate cognitive impairment. While it was obvious early on that something was wrong, the diagnosis of PWS, in Stuart's case, did not happen until my sister Mary happened to read an article on Prader-Willi sometime in the early 1970s. Stuart was about five feet tall and his weight varied from two hundred to three hundred pounds. For the seventh child of an active family, to be born with such a handicap was extremely trying.

Stuart driving Mitzi with Charlotte, c. 1956

Yet a calendar my sister Betsy sent out shows Stuart astride Winnie, my mother's Welsh pony, in 1957, and a photograph of all the children taken about the same time, pictures Stuart on skis.

I remember the day my mother brought Stuart home from the hospital. To me, aged nine, he looked like all the other babies my mother had brought home—small, helpless, and crying. But my parents knew something was wrong, as did the doctors, and the prognosis was that he might live to age twenty, or perhaps thirty. No one knew. No one expected him to live as long as he did.

It is difficult to imagine what Stuart's young life outside of home had to have been like. He attended a small private school in Peterborough, the Gosling School, run by a Miss Lindeman. That he was teased and tormented we know, but not to what extent. What is more important is that, as he got older, he found outlets in art, in the goats he raised, and among the thousands of books he owned and read. The psychological scars he carried got the best of him from time to time, but the remarkable thing is that his art, for the most part, expresses sensitivity, joy, and a love for life.

As mentioned, many of Stuart's paintings include a bright yellow

sun, to me a symbol of happiness. Most
are playful and joyful. His paintings also
reflect his travels, which he loved. Twice
he went to Africa, once in 1977 with my
sister Jenny (who was the closest of all
the siblings to Stuart) and again in 1980.
Thus his collection includes many works
with wild animals. Jenny also took him
to Switzerland in 1971, and again the
trip provided him subject matter. Texas,

Stuart with Indy, 1957

where he lived for the last four-and-a-half years, gave him a new back-
drop, and he continued to draw and paint until very late in his life. Most
of his work was done in permanent markers and oil-pastel crayons.

Many of his paintings were titled, with short explanations. One that
hangs in my house is of Canadian geese: "We honk with joy, swimming
near the bank of the marsh where the wildflowers are in full bloom. We
have hatched five babies." A painting he did after returning from Africa
shows a crocodile and is captioned with a double entendre: "I will wait
until some sucker comes along. I hope it's a gnu this time." Another is
entitled "Motherhood." Underneath, the inscription reads: "The mother
doe is telling its fawn to stay hidden while she goes off to feed." And
another that depicts a horse and a swarm of bumblebees: "Galloping
through the wildflowers, stumbled upon a honeybee's nest." The bees
are happily buzzing about, while the horse, startled, gallops off.

Besides his paintings, Stuart produced at least one set of postcards
and, during the 1970s, at least three calendars. One of my favorites is
the picture for July 1976, entitled "Taking Over the World." A clothed
horse is driving a naked man. The caption underneath concludes: "The
horse is holding a whip over the man's head. This is what will happen if
the animals take over the world." What a perfect illustration for George
Orwell's *Animal Farm*!

Stuart had a number of exhibits. A special one was a joint exhibition at the English Gallery in Peterborough with our mother. While the

Stuart (with Betsy) on Mitzi, 1953

exhibit was a big success, my mother's death a few days later depressed Stuart deeply. When, shortly afterwards, he was asked to do a solo exhibition in Keene, New Hampshire, he at first declined. A few months later he agreed. And in a spurt of creativity, he produced as many as four paintings a day, explaining that he was "frolicking" and "could not stop." Outside of New Hampshire, his work has been shown at galleries in Boston and New York, and his pieces are part of the permanent display at the Currier Museum in Manchester, New Hampshire. A mural he did for a social service agency in Keene was removed and is now on permanent display at the Monadnock Children's Museum.

Sheldon Tarakan, former publisher of *Prader-Willi Perspectives,* interviewed Stuart twenty years ago and described his artistic genius: "It lies in his ability to give each animal a life, which is uniquely intertwined with his own fantasies; a life which exists somewhere 'over the rainbow' and not in the veldt or the barnyard; a life which has a unique meaning and message for each viewer."

Several months before Stuart's death, my brother Frank engaged

Stuart with one of his paintings, December 1990

William Corbett, a founder of The Pressed Wafer, a specialized publisher. Frank asked him to produce a book of Stuart's work. Mr. Corbett
visited Stuart in Texas and was planning another trip. While it is disap-
pointing that Stuart did not live to see the book published, it will prove
a fitting memorial to a talented artist when it is printed.

Our parents raised goats from their earliest married days, but they
held a special place for Stuart. He often named them after family members. At home, I have a 50,000-word manuscript of Stuart's entitled
Gisela My Friend. The story is about a three-teated nanny goat that Stuart bought in the early 1970s and her integration into the family of goats
he already owned. It's a lively and sensitive depiction of goat life. There
is joy in the birth of new kids, and tears when one of his favorites dies.
There is combativeness as goats play "king of the mountain," humor in
goats prancing atop the roof of the veterinarian's car, and poignancy, as
Stuart holds his dying goat Kathe, as she expires in his arms.

Stuart was an exceptional reader. He had a few thousand books, most
of them dealing with animals and natural history, and, unlike some peo-

One of Stuart's paintings

ple, he had read most of them. Many were first editions, including a collection of all of Alfred Payson Terhune's dog stories. While Stuart had a hard time articulating his thoughts—his handicap, at times, frustrated him enormously—his comprehension was remarkable. He could talk about books he had read and authors he admired for hours.

Stuart's life was filled with much else. He was always a big fan of country and western music. My sisters Charlotte and Jenny took him to a Willie Nelson concert on his sixtieth birthday. He sat, as he always did, in the front row, clapping his hands and jumping to his feet. He went home with a photograph of himself with Willie, where it joined similar photographs of him with Dolly Parton and Loretta Lynn. In 1988, Jenny and Charlotte took Stuart to the Grand Ole Opry, a never-forgotten experience for Stuart. Living in Texas, he took a greater interest in religion and at one point considered being re-baptized by being dunked in a river. He must have reconsidered, for it never happened.

He loved to go for drives. He often sat in the back seat and would direct the driver away from Abilene, which was where he lived in Texas. He preferred the less-traveled roads, and trips of several hours, during which sleep was a frequent companion, were a pleasure to him. Though he didn't swim much in Texas, he used to love it. It gave him a physical freedom that eluded him on land. He would float peacefully for hours.

However, all was not peaceful in Stuart's life. Once, before our mother died, he had to be taken to the hospital in the middle of the night. He had become very heavy and had difficulty breathing. He spent several days in intensive care. During the dark days following the death of our mother—and it was Stuart who found her dead in her bed—he was institutionalized twice. For a short while, his art took on a darker, more ominous tone. Then in 2010, he was hospitalized again. The outlook was dire. As his siblings, we were asked the extent to which the doctors should go to keep him alive. Surprising everyone, including his doctors, he survived and thrived.

December 2, his birthday, held both joy and fright for Stuart. It was the date on which our father died in 1968 at the age of fifty-eight—the day Stuart turned eighteen. Our mother told him that made it a very special day. But then, twenty-two years later, our mother died on the same day. A few years later his dog Simon was hit by a car and killed on December 2. And then, when one would think Stuart needed no more punishing reminders, our sister Mary died on December 3, 1997, like our father of cancer and also at the age of fifty-eight.

But his ability to recover seemed miraculous. He lived to create, and he maintained a disposition that most of us strive to achieve; the legacy he left has been the joy so many of us get from viewing his delightful works of art.

Remarkably, Stuart's art triumphed over the demons that sometimes took control of his life; it transcends this life and anything that comes afterwards. With his bright yellow suns, he depicts a view of the world that sends scurrying the black clouds of despair that we know periodically enveloped him.

Albert Einstein once wrote: "There are only two ways to live your life. One is as though nothing is a miracle. The other is as though everything is a miracle." Who would ever have thought that Stuart, burdened as he was with the incapacitating effects of Prader-Willi, would have so much in common with the German physicist who developed the Theory of Relativity?

In the end, my mother was right. December 2 will always be a special day, for it is the day that gave us Stuart.

The Toadstool

Some books are to be tasted, others to be swallowed, and some few to be chewed and digested.

Francis Bacon (1561–1626)
The Advancement of Learning, 1605

A man ought to read just as inclination leads him; for what he reads as a task will do him little good.

Samuel Johnson (1709–1784)
James Boswell, *Life of Johnson*, 1791

The toad beneath the harrow knows
Exactly where each tooth-point goes;
The butterfly upon the road
Preaches contentment to that toad.

Rudyard Kipling (1832–1898)
"Paget, MP" 1886

TOADSTOOL IS A FITTING NAME FOR A BOOKSTORE. One envisions a secluded, earthy, enchanted place, forested with toadstools under which elves recline engrossed in books. One evening in late 1971 or early 1972 several of us siblings gathered at our mother's house to discuss the prospect of a bookstore. Normally, family conversations resembled the incoherence of a bunch of Parliament backbenchers with everybody speaking at the same time, but this time we stayed on subject. As my brother Willard recalls, another brother, Frank, first mentioned the name "Toadstool." However, as Willard points out, there was ". . . what I think was a subliminal understanding of the name based on the cover illustration of *The Golden Book of Fairy Tales*"—a book all of us had read and one that Willard owns today with a cover depicting elves, engrossed in books, sitting under toadstools. So, in one of those marvelous happenings, which are not just coincidence, the name of the bookstore was derived from a book. The store opened in our hometown of Peterborough in early May of 1972. Willard, nineteen at the time and

Sarah Moody, Betsy's daughter, on a toadstool at the Toadstool

having recently completed his freshman year at Prescott College in Arizona, and our sister Jenny, then twenty-three and recently graduated from Sweet Briar College, were in charge.

With $25,000 in capital, the business commenced. Eight hundred square feet were leased in the Centertown Building at 3 Main Street. Shelves were constructed and stocked with 10,000 titles. Prior to opening, the cash register was placed in the center of the store on the assumption, as Willard said, if you show people trust, they will be honest with you. An opening-night party was held for family and close friends. The next morning an inventory was conducted. Three books were missing. The cash register was moved to the front of the store—a relatively inexpensive lesson in retailing.

Willard and his wife Holly, at the Toadstool in Peterborough

Peterborough today has a population of 6,000, but back in 1972 it was closer to 3,000, not much larger than it had been 100 years earlier. Despite its small size, the village is the commercial hub for half a dozen surrounding towns. The town boasts the first free public library in the United States and was part of the route of the Underground Railway. Frederick Douglass spent a night at the Moses Cheney house, once a stop on the road to freedom for a number of enslaved Americans.

The town has long had an artistic population. The MacDowell Colony began operations in 1907 and is very much alive today. Marian MacDowell established the Colony to honor her husband Edward MacDowell (1860–1908), a composer and pianist who had been seriously injured a few years earlier. Alan Seeger, Padraic Colum, Edwin Arlington Robinson, James Baldwin, Alice Walker, Dubose Heyward, Aaron Copland, and Leonard Bernstein are among a host of artists, musicians, poets, and writers who spent time at the MacDowell Colony. Thornton Wilder wrote *Our Town* at the Colony in 1937. Grover's Corners is the name of the town in the play, but the stage manager mentions all the towns which surround Peterborough; Grover's Corners is an amalgamation of those small villages. Peterborough has also long been a summer home to residents of Boston. As early as 1851, when rail service first reached East Wilton, New Hampshire (two towns to the east), one could leave Boston at noon, travel by train to Wilton, and by stage coach to Peterborough and arrive by 5 o'clock in the evening—about twice as long as the trip takes today.[3] The town has been home to a good number of academics and literary types. For example, Professors Elting Morison (American history), Harlow Shapley (astronomy), and Vannevar Bush (atomic energy), all had summer homes in the immediate vicinity, as did scientist and inventor, Edwin H. Land (Polaroid). Authors Elizabeth Yates, Newt Tolman, Haydn Pearson, and Elizabeth Thomas lived or live in the area; as did (and do) poets Allan Block, John Martin, Marianne Moore, and Julia Older, along with illustrators Nora Unwin and Wallace Tripp. In the 1920s, Paul Robeson and Bette Davis performed and Martha Graham danced at the Mariarden Arts Colony. The Peterborough Players, a summer theatre, opened in the 1930s and brought many well-known plays and talented actors and actresses to the area. Growing up I recall seeing plays such as *The Philadelphia Story*, *The Matchmaker*, *The Diary of Anne Frank,* and *The Devil and Daniel Webster*. In 2007, James Whitmore returned in a role he had originally played at the Peterborough Players in 1956—Sheridan Whiteside in *The Man Who Came to Dinner.*

With such a rich artistic heritage, it is not surprising that Peterborough was and is a fruitful place for a bookstore. Willard, with the confidence of youth, stated in a 1992 interview, "We had no vision of failure." During that first partial year the store generated about $25,000 in revenues and $40,000 in the first full year. In the early days Willard and Jenny paid themselves $10 a day and so the store was profitable from the start—perhaps a good lesson for many of today's budding

---

3 *History of Peterborough, New Hampshire,* 1954, George Abbot Morrison.

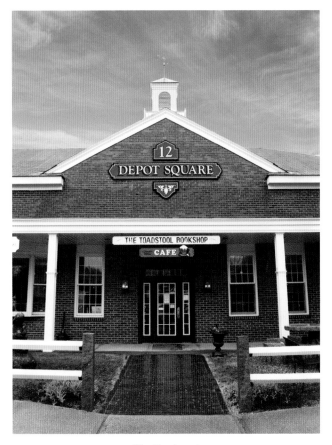

The Toadstool

entrepreneurs, many of whom seem anxious to prematurely take their businesses public. Willard's original plan was to return to college, but like the Jimmy Stewart character, George Bailey, in *It's a Wonderful Life*, he found himself inextricably enmeshed in the business. Over the next few years The Toadstool doubled its square footage. Each year's sales exceeded the previous year's and profitability persisted. Early on Willard was conscious of the rising trend toward superstores. He deliberately avoided competing with them, but, like them, kept building his inventory and looking to expand. His target town was a smaller place with characteristics similar to those of Peterborough. In 1983 he opened a second store in Keene, a community of 22,000 and the home of Keene State College. However, he decided not to open a store in West Lebanon, New Hampshire, because of its proximity to Hanover and the Dartmouth College bookstore. Around 1984, Jenny, whose first love has always been horses, left to teach riding and skiing full time. Willard, today, credits her with much of their early success. At about the same time, Willard's wife Holly began spending more time in the store. Today she does much of the buying, and her knowledge of customer wants keeps the shelves filled with appropriate titles.

In 1989 a third store opened in Milford, New Hampshire, about twenty miles to the east. Eye-balling Willard's success, Barnes and Noble, in 1990, opened a store in Manchester about fifteen miles east of Milford and Borders opened a store in Keene in 1992. In spite of this competition The Toadstool's inventory of books and attractive layout continues to attract customers. In 1992 Willard moved the flagship store to its current location, a 7,500-square-foot former A&P supermarket in Depot Square and increased the inventory from 30,000 books to 70,000. The building was owned by Yankee Publications, and The Toadstool became the sole lessee. A few months later, amidst a recession and at Willard's price, The Toadstool purchased the property.

Today the three Toadstool stores carry a collective inventory of just under 300,000 books. Each one offers comfortable chairs. Aesop's Tables leases space and operates a café in the Peterborough store, and the shop in Keene is located in the Colony Mill Marketplace with a food court downstairs. All the staff is knowledgeable and friendly. The sense of enchantment originally envisioned is present in each store. While one may not see elves lurking beneath toadstools, many of the patrons can be found comfortably ensconced in nooks, quietly leafing through books. Despite the advent of Amazon and electronic books, customers continue to come through the doors. In 1992, Willard was interviewed by Elizabeth Yates for *The Peterborough Transcript*. The eighty-seven-year-old Ms. Yates was the author of over forty books including *Amos*

Fortune, Free Man, which won the Newbery medal in 1951. During the course of the interview Willard asked her a question: "What do you think the future will bring for readers, for writers, for literature, for the art of writing?" Elizabeth Yates replied, "The book speaks to the mind in a manner that elicits response. As the speed and pressure of life increase, so will the need for books and solace, delight, and inspiration." There is little doubt in my mind that The Toadstool will continue to thrive.

From a $25,000 investment, Willard created a business that over its life has generated in excess of $50,000,000 in revenues, sells close to $5,000,000 worth of books annually (that's about $175.00 per square foot), employs 40 people, and has a book value of $2,500,000. The Toadstool has paid out $75,000 in dividends and has retired one share (four percent of shares outstanding) for $80,000. Book value of the business has compounded at 14.2 percent for 35 years, almost twice that of the Dow Jones Industrial Average. Today Willard sits on an advisory board of the American Booksellers Association and was Business Leader of the Year in Peterborough in 1998. Most importantly he has provided himself and his family a good living doing what he loves. Willa Cather, another author who lived in the neighboring town of Jaffrey, once wrote, "Where there is great love there are always miracles." The Toadstool qualifies. As Willard's older brother, my pride knows no bounds and, as a shareholder, I am deeply satisfied.

My library at Old Lyme, with a bust of me by my father

Books

Once, when I asked him why he got
So many books, he said, "why not?"
I've puzzled over that a lot.

Jane, Joseph and John: Their Book of Verses, c. 1918
Ralph Bergengren (1871–1947)

BOOKS HAVE LONG BEEN INTEGRAL to my life. Growing up in Peterborough, my parents' bookshelves were filled with many wonderful titles, mostly inherited from their parents. As a young child, my mother would read nursery stories, along with tales from the Brothers Grimm, Beatrix Potter, and Thornton W. Burgess. As I grew older, I recall reading such stories as William McCleery's *The Wolf Story*, Haydn Pearson's *That Darned Minister's Son*, Anna Sewell's *Black Beauty*, the stories of Jack London, and E.B. White's *Stuart Little* and *Charlotte's Web*. At age twelve I received a copy of *The House on the Cliff* by Fentin W. Dixon and so was introduced to the Hardy boys. I proceeded to read the entire series. Books that have remained favorites include novels such as Pearl Buck's *The Good Earth*, Trygve Gulbranssen's *Beyond Sing the Woods,* and O.E. Rolvaag's *Giants in the Earth*, among many others. Bertie Wooster, Jeeves, Uncle Fred, Clarence, Aunt Agatha, Mr. Mulliner, and a number of others all became friends when I discovered the humor and lively imagination of the Edwardian world depicted by P.G. Wodehouse. (And they have remained so through the Drones, a small group of Wodehouse devotees, who meet irregularly in New York).

Among the classics I read as a teenager were *David Copperfield, Jane Eyre*, and *Pride and Prejudice*. The history of England came alive in the children's history of that "emerald island" written simply and lovingly by H. E. Marshall in *An Island Story*. My copy is the one my parents had, printed in 1920 by Frederick A. Stokes in New York. It was recently reprinted, so I snapped up three copies for my children. The history of the United States was made vivid with Mason Weems' description of George

Washington and the cherry tree, and then, earnestly, when I picked up and read Carl Sandberg's biography of Lincoln, *Abraham Lincoln: The Prairie Years* and *Abraham Lincoln: The War Years.* I have copies of most of these books in my library today and have re-read a number of them, in some cases more than once. The great beauty of these stories is that the characters they portray and the morals they impart are universal and so are as relevant today as they were when written.

My academic career suffered a prolonged adolescence. Other than a high school English teacher (Horace E. Thorner at Williston Academy in East Hampton, Massachusetts), whose concentration on Shakespeare was such that the two plays which we read my junior year—*Macbeth* and *Hamlet*—remain etched in my memory fifty years later, I fell victim to the many distractions of mid- and late-teenage years. It was some time before I focused again on books. But then fate stepped into my path. In 1967, married for three years with a one-year-old son and my wife pregnant with our daughter, we moved into a delightful eighteenth-century house in Durham, Connecticut, fortuitously situated close by a pleasant, retired couple, Keith and Helena Hutchison. Keith, a retired editor with *The Nation,* was the proprietor of the Durham Book Service, dealers in old books. In him I found a spark which reignited my dormant interest. In me he found a willing student and customer. My addictions, again, became literary. Keith was almost blind, British, and a staunch liberal Democrat. He had attended the London School of Economics and worked for Clement Atlee in the general election of 1922, but soon left politics and, in his writing career, concentrated on economics. Among the books he wrote is *Rival Powers, America and Britain in the Postwar World*, a signed first printing of which sits on my shelves today. His love for books led him to start a small business selling books, particularly to libraries. His search for books of an economic nature would often cause him to buy entire libraries, including a number of novels. From Keith I bought several wonderful first editions, all of which I still have—books such as Isak Dinesen's *Out of Africa* (bought for $3.00); Laurence Housman's *Palace Plays* ($2.75); William Gerhardi's *Memoirs of a Polyglot*

Grandson Alex Williams at age 2

($3.00); Lucretia Hale's *The Peterkin Papers* ($25.00); Stephen Crane's *The Red Badge of Courage* ($5.00); Frances Hodgson Burnett's *Little Lord Fauntleroy* ($37.50), and Mark Twain's *Huckleberry Finn* ($150.00). When, after four years, we left Durham for Greenwich, Keith gave me his copy of John Carter's *Carter's ABC for Book Collectors*. It sits today on my shelves among a collection of books about books.

During those years in Durham I visited William Reese in New Haven, from whom I bought a few books, and I began receiving catalogues from Goodspeed's in Boston and Brentano's in New York. Brentano's rare book department closed after a few years, but when it was open I took advantage of their offerings. Taking every dollar I could scrounge, I bought nicely bound sets of Dickens, Jane Austen, and the Bronte sisters; a beautifully bound first edition of *Zulieka Dobson* ($46.00) by Max Beerbohm; the trilogy of the breakfast table—all first editions—by Oliver Wendell Holmes ($175.00 for the three volumes), the first volume of which, *The Autocrat at the Breakfast Table,* includes a signed letter from Mr. Holmes; and a first edition of *Uncle Tom's Cabin* ($350.00) that included a letter from its author, Harriet Beecher Stowe.

Goodspeed's Book Shop at the top of Beacon Hill had been around for

My library in Old Lyme. "John Bull' is by James Pritchard of Peterborough.
The bust on the windowsill is of my mother by my father, c. 1937

many years. They specialized in genealogy and town histories, but they also sold well-known (and lesser-known) books. Town histories have always interested me, and I bought volumes dealing with all the towns in which I had lived. I also acquired a number of books dealing with the genealogy of my family and my wife's family. But my greatest pleasure was in finding copies of books I had known and loved as a youngster. From Goodspeed's I bought a copy of Joel Chandler Harris's *Daddy Jake the Runaway* for $50.00 in 1971, and six years later added *Uncle Remus* for $150.00. Other books I bought from them include Robert Frost's *A Further Range* ($15.00); P.G. Wodehouse's *My Man Jeeves* ($50.00); A. A. Milne's *Winnie the Pooh* ($25.00), and the first whaling novel published in the United States, Joseph Hart's *Miriam Coffin* ($150.00). Through my grandfather I had learned of John Kendrick Bangs, who was best known for *Houseboat on the River Styx,* published in 1896. He was a prolific author and I have twenty of his titles today, most purchased during that same period for less than $5.00 from the Gotham Book Mart in Manhattan. Their store on West 47th Street used to have a sign stating, "Wise Men Fish Here"—a sign I would have paid dearly for. I rarely see Bangs for sale today, but that has less to do with their scarcity (they were printed in large numbers) than their desirability.

In 1971 we moved to Greenwich where, within a few years, I met David Block who had just left his "real" job to open a bookstore, The Book Block, on West Putnam Avenue. David was only there a short time before moving the operation to his home in Cos Cob where he came to specialize in Americana, becoming one of the foremost dealers in the nation. His wife Shiu-Min is a bookbinder—the best that I know—who not only repairs books, but who also builds boxes for books. One of my favorites is a silk-lined, three-quarter-bound red leather box she built to house a copy of Nien Cheng's *Life and Death in Shanghai,* which Ms. Cheng presented to me in 1990. Over the years Shiu-Min has probably repaired and built boxes for a hundred of my books.

When David first opened the store he sold anything he found of interest. Early on, I received a call from him saying that he had come across about twenty-five Wodehouse first editions. The asking price of $250 seemed steep, so I asked two friends, Gerry Gold and Ed LeGard, if we might form a syndicate to buy the collection. They agreed and we did. Over the years I bought some wonderful items from David, including a copy of E.B. White's *Charlotte's Web* ($140.00); the December 1863 edition of *The Atlantic Monthly,* which included the first publication of Edward Everett Hale's *The Man Without a Country* ($375.00); two copies of *Webster's Dictionary,* published in 1828; a letter from Noah Webster in which he refers to Henry Trowbridge, my great-great-grandfather who married Webster's granddaughter; and a copy of *Through the Looking Glass,* presented by Lewis Carroll to Edith Rose Blakemore in 1878. Edith was one of a number of young girls Charles Dodgson had known in

Oxford when he wrote *Alice in Wonderland.*

I continue to buy books (admittedly at a lesser rate, as prices have soared), though at times paying prices that shock my native New England sensibilities. Among a host of dealers I find informative, fair, and honorable are Nigel Williams, Adrian Harrington, and John Suamarez Smith of Heywood Hill in London; Charles Gould in Maine; Peter Stern and the Boston Book Company in Boston; and Robert Dagg and Thomas Goldwasser in San Francisco. Catalogues continue to clog my mailbox and provide pleasurable and informative reading. However, my preference is to find authors I like whose books are reasonably priced—writers such as Beverly Nichols, George MacDonald Fraser, Jonathon Ames, John Mortimer, James Salter, and Louis Begley. I agree with Otto Penzler, proprietor of the Mysterious Bookshop in Manhattan and author of "The Crime Scene," a weekly column in *The New York Sun,* when he writes that some of the best fiction today is written by mystery writers, authors like Charles McCarry, John Dunning, Sarah Caudwell, Alan Furst, and Robert Barnard. So I frequent book fairs in New York and out-of-the-way bookshops in search of a prize or for the sheer pleasure of being among books. My collection is a nice one, but has no extraordinary value except to me. The Wodehouse collection is reasonably large (about four hundred items), but is missing a few items and I have close to one hundred books relating to the American Civil War. I have never collected with the idea that my books would have great value, and I don't presume they do, though the compounded returns (based upon catalogue prices) have been generous; the original investments were pretty small. But the joy they have given me is real.

In 1967, I bought a 1921 first edition of *A Magnificent Farce,* written by A. Edward Newton from Keith Hutchison. I paid $5.00. In the book, Mr. Newton writes a sentiment that could serve as mine: "I early formed the habit of buying books, and, thank God, I have never lost it."

Remembering December 2

I am the Alpha and the Omega, the beginning and the end, the first and the last.
Book of Revelation 22:13

And in the end, it is not the years in your life that count. It is the life in your years.
Abraham Lincoln (1809–1865)

DECEMBER 2 IS A DATE TO REMEMBER. On this date in 1763, the first synagogue in what would become the United States was built—Touro Synagogue in, of all places, Newport, Rhode Island. Shabbat services are still held on Friday evenings and on Saturday mornings. On December 2, 1804, Napoleon had himself crowned Emperor of France. John Brown was hanged on this date in 1859 for leading a raid against the United States arsenal at Harper's Ferry, in what would be a precursor of the Civil War. It was also on this date in 1942, under the stands at Stagg Field at the University of Chicago, that Enrico Fermi produced the first controlled nuclear fission chain reaction, and the atomic age was born. And on December 2, 1981, Britney Spears was born.

For me, my family, and my siblings, however, December 2 has very special meaning. The day has meant birth and it has brought death.

It was on this date that my brother Stuart was born in 1950. The seventh of nine children, Stuart was born with a condition—at the time unidentified—now known as Prader-Willi Syndrome. Prader-Willi is a rare genetic disorder, in which seven genes on chromosome fifteen are deleted or unexpressed in the paternal chromosome. The disorder affects approximately one in every eighteen thousand births. It was first described in 1956 by Andrea Prader and Heinrich Willi and a team of researchers in Switzerland. The syndrome is accompanied with an insatiable appetite and manifests itself in obesity, small stature, delayed puberty, small hands and feet, and some learning disorders. There is no known cure.

Stuart handled the cards he was dealt with a remarkable resilience, good humor, and a sense of independence unexpected in one so afflicted. He lived with my mother until her death, and then lived in Texas about a hundred miles west of Dallas. He read more than most people I know and pursued a career as an artist, following in the steps of our parents.

December 2 was also the date on or practically on which three people very close to me died—my father, my mother, and sister. My father died in 1968, at fifty-eight, after a ten-month bout with lung cancer that had metastasized to his brain. My mother died at seventy-nine during the night of December 2–December 3 twenty-two years later, in 1990. (Stuart, who was the only one home at the time, is certain she died on December 2. If that date was good enough for Stuart, it is good enough for me.) My sister Mary died, like my father, at age fifty-eight on the morning of December 3, 1997, after a five-year battle with breast cancer and bone cancer.

So, to me and my family, December 2nd and the days surrounding it are exceptional—a time for remembrance. It marks the Alpha and Omega of life. After my father's death, on Stuart's eighteenth birthday, my mother, in comforting Stuart who felt terribly about the timing (and my mother little realizing the importance the date would play in her life), stressed the special meaning the date would always hold.

Stuart's birth gave life to a wonderful, creative man whose art now hangs in museums and who, in the manner in which he handled his disabilities, inspired all who know him. The deaths of my parents and my sister, all of whom died too early but all of whom took Lincoln's words as their maxim, serve as a reminder of the sweetness of life and the importance of living well each day. All four live on in memory.

Sixty-Nine Years on Skis

Skiing is a dance and the mountain always leads.

IN MY BARN IN OLD LYME, Connecticut, hang a pair of Stein Eriksens, skis that were given to me when I turned fifteen in 1956. At the time, they were state of the art with a black-and-white laminated top and multi-grooved base. At 214 centimeters, they are roughly one-third longer than the skis I use today. The toe binding was designed with a clasp that, when pushed forward, levered your boot back; the heels were held down by a six-foot leather strap called a "long thong," which was anchored to the base of the ski and wrapped around your boot to hold it firmly in place. The bindings that clamped the front of the boot were, for obvious reasons, called "bear traps." In 1956, the skis cost my parents $85; the comparable price today would be about $700.

~

My first skis appeared on Christmas 1944. With my father headed to Italy with the ski troops, my mother, who was not a skier, decided the gift was appropriate. We had moved temporarily from New Hampshire to her parents' home in East River, Connecticut, but fortunately there was enough snow on the ground that I was able to walk around. So began a lifetime love affair with the sport.

When we returned to Peterborough after the war, my father took my sister, brother, and me to Whit's Tow, located just north of the village on Middle Hancock Road, the road on which we lived. Skiers gripped Mr. Whitcomb's rope tow and it carried them four- or five-hundred feet to a point on the edge of the Peterborough Golf Club. While skiers today would thumb their nose at Whit's, the hill offered a nearby opportunity to learn to ski.

Me, 1960

The rope ascended what seemed a steep pitch and then flattened as it neared the top. The rope became very heavy as it went over the crest and was ideal for "snapping off" girls (or our teachers) who might be riding behind. The idea was, once over the crest, to swing out to the left several feet and let the rope go. It would snake back sinuously, making it almost impossible for those hanging on behind to remain upright. By the time the victims had picked themselves up, we were back at the bottom of the hill, our faces angelic, as we gripped the rope for the next trip.

∼

Nick Paumgarten, in a piece entitled "The Ski Gods" (*The New Yorker,* March 15, 2010), writes that archeological finds in Norway indicate that skiing goes back thousands of years: "Skis predate the wheel; we ripped before we rolled," he wrote. In America, skiing was introduced early in the twentieth century. One of the early promoters was the Dartmouth Outing Club, founded in 1909. During the next ten years, Dartmouth men skied forty miles to Mt. Moosilauke, a 4,802-foot peak where the college owns 4,600 acres (about a third of the mountain above 2,000 feet). They climbed Mt. Washington and, with Carl Shumway as the president of the club, were the first on skis into Tuckerman's Ravine on March 9, 1913.

The 1920s saw more skiers take up the sport, including Al Sise of Wellesley, Massachusetts, (formerly of Vermont), whose daughter, Nancy, I once raced. Al Sise had the longest racing career on record, from 1928 until 1981. A "snow train" would leave Boston's North Station, taking skiers to Pinkham Notch, New Hampshire. In the very early 1930s, my father, then in college, could take an early morning train, ski on Mt. Washington, and return the same day, or the next, in time for a hearty dinner at Durgin-Park Restaurant.

Skiing expanded in popularity during the 1930s, but, given the depressed economy, it remained a "rich man's sport." Those two decades, between the end of World War I and the start of World War II, saw a number of accomplished European skiers, like Austrians Hannes Schneider and Toni Matt, escape the Nazis and come to this country.

~

The "big" hill locally was Temple Mountain, near the town line between Peterborough and Temple. This area had perhaps twice the vertical drop as Whit's and was owned and operated by Charlie Beebe, a classmate of my father's from Harvard. It was there, on New Year's Eve 1961, that my sister, Mary, introduced me to Caroline, the girl who would become my wife.

It was also at Temple that I first used my Stein Eriksens. Eriksen was born in Norway in 1927 and won a gold medal in giant slalom at the 1952 Olympics, becoming the first skier not from the Alps so honored. Following the Olympics, he moved to the United States and is director of skiing at the Deer Valley Resort and host of the Stein Eriksen Lodge. At the age of 89, he continues to ski.

The heavy black skis with their distinctive four white grooves on top—two in front and two behind—were fast and the envy of my friends. My first races were on those skis and later, in 1958, on a pair of Kästles. Anton Kästle made his first pair of skis in 1924 in Austria; by the mid 1950s they became the favored skis of those on the World Tour and, in fact, every member of the 1956 U.S. Olympic ski team used Kästles.

My Kästles Kombinations, with their marker bindings, also hang in my barn, the now-frayed leather long thongs still attached. These were the skis I used in the late 1950s during a downhill race on Mount Sunapee's Flying Goose. Sunapee is a state-owned property about forty miles north of Peterborough. The race was one in a series for those competing in the Eastern Juniors. The area was served by a single chairlift, but as racers we had to walk up the course carrying our skis, so as to better learn its turns and its contours. It was during this hike up that I realized my racing career would be short, for "discretion in the face of fear" is a motto to which I ascribe. In those days a downhill race consisted of a starting point and a finish gate. There were no control gates. The fastest skier down the hill won. As we walked up the Flying Goose, I noted some of the boys marking trees, so they could cut corners by skiing through the woods. I thought they were crazy and I have no memory as to who won the race, other than it wasn't me.

～

It was about that same time that my father took my brother Frank and me to Tuckerman's Ravine on Mt. Washington, a place my father first skied in the late 1920s. We stayed at the Lodge at Pinkham Notch, now designated the Joe Dodge Lodge—somewhat enlarged, but looking pretty much the same. At that time, Joe Dodge was the proprietor. His son, Brooks, skied for Dartmouth and in the 1956 Olympics. The base of the Tuckerman's Ravine is about two-and-a-half miles up from Pinkham Notch. We put seal skins on the bottoms of our skis; the fur reversed allowing one to glide forward, but preventing the skis from sliding backward. Releasing the cable bindings allowed one to lift one's heel making the ascension easier. The climb up took a couple of hours.

My first view of Tuckerman's was breathtaking. It resembles one-third of an enormous bowl, stretching about a mile from one side to the other. The snow reaches depths of about one hundred feet. One climbs

Me, in "China Bowl" at Vail, 2004

over the "little headwall" and into the bowl, where there are no trees and only a couple of large rocks; the one on the right was known as the "lunch rock." Facing the ravine on the right is Lion's Head Trail; on the left is Boot Spur.

The air was crisp and cool, the sky blue. Distant skiers appeared as black specks against the snow-white background. The slope begins gradually before steepening sharply as it terminates at the "lip." As you walk up carrying your skis, you can stretch out your arm and touch the slope in front of you. While I never skied over the lip of the headwall (I climbed to a point just under it), I could see the two rocks you had to avoid when skiing off the top. One of America's most famous early races was called The Inferno; it went from the top of Mt. Washington to the

Pinkham Notch Lodge, a distance of four miles. And the most famous of the Inferno races occurred in 1939 when Toni Matt, an Austrian skier, *schussed* the headwall in poor visibility conditions. His time was just over six-and-a-half minutes, eclipsing the skier who placed second by six full minutes. It has been estimated that he must have hit speeds of eighty-five miles per hour as he came over the headwall and down the ravine—an unbelievable feat in those days and on that equipment.

We had time for three runs on the headwall, eating a packed lunch on the lunch rock before heading back down. The next day, across Pinkham Notch, we climbed Wildcat Trail, which had been cut by the Civilian Conservation Corps in 1933. Another of my father's classmates, Bob Livermore, who in 1931 had been the first to ski over the lip of Tuckerman's ravine, won the first race down its slope in 1934. On March 12, 1962, my wife-to-be broke her leg on Wildcat Mountain, as she and I headed down on our first (and last) run of the day—her last time on downhill skis.

⌒

Despite my mediocre performance racing in the Eastern Junior races, I joined the ski team at Williston Academy in 1956, becoming its captain in my second year. The school had a ski area on the west slope of Mt. Tom that was serviced by a rope tow. We had to participate in all four skiing disciplines—downhill, slalom, cross-country, and jumping. I liked downhill and slalom. Cross-country was too much like work. Jumping, however, was totally new to me. The skis were longer, wider, and heavier than regular skis, with four or five grooves on the bottom for stabilization. The school had a small, perhaps twenty-meter, jump, reached by climbing a steep pitch. You slid back down, then over a man-made lip, landing on a second steep slope. My first time down I attempted to jump, sprang forward at the edge of the jump, somersaulted, and landed on the back of my neck. I slid down the hill, frustrated and chagrined, but unhurt. The next time I just coasted off the jump. Fortunately, during my three years at the school, we never had to jump in competition.

Most of our meets were held at similarly skier-challenged and snow-deprived schools. I remember one multi-school meet on Mt. Greylock in Williamstown, MA. It was snowing and visibility was poor. I was slotted to be the first racer down. One of the forerunners had a bad accident in the descent and the race was called. Fortunately the young man was not seriously hurt; relieved, I skied slowly and carefully to the bottom.

∽

During the mid to late 1950s, my father began taking us further afield— day trips to Mount Sunapee, Hogback Mountain, and Mt. Snow, and overnight ones to Stowe, Mad River Glen, and Cannon Mountain. Mt. Snow was a more recent ski resort. Walter Schoenknecht, a tall, slope-shouldered man, came to Vermont in about 1955 from Mohawk Mountain in Connecticut. When we first went there Mr. Schoenknecht was always around, asking how everybody was; he knew us by name. Since my father usually had four to six children in tow, we were a memorable and recognizable sight. Hogback Mountain, which opened in 1946, was unusual in that the parking area was midway up the slope, so you skied down to buy your ticket and at the end of the day you took the T-bar up to the top and skied back to your car. On warm, early spring days, when maple sap was flowing, those waiting in line were served maple taffy on snow.

Stowe was exciting and glamorous with people arriving from all over the east coast. A single chairlift served Mt. Mansfield; so on very nice days during holiday weekends, the wait in line could take up to an hour. But the length and steepness of the trails justified the wait. At the top was the Octagon, which served hamburgers that were overpriced at fifty cents. The Nose Dive, with its seven turns, was the oldest, trickiest, and best-known trail. It started slightly above the top of the lift and was narrow and steep. On icy days it was treacherous. I remember once, on a very icy day, watching in awe as Christian Pravda, a dual-medalist in the 1952 Olympics, swooped down like a giant bird. The other trail at Stowe that I remember well was the steep and wide National. Once on the National, with visibility so poor that you could only see a few feet up or down the slope, a skier appeared out of the fog—and then disappeared like a phantom. It was Marvin Moriarty, a member of the 1956 U.S. Olympic team. It was on the National on another trip, that my father was finally forced to replace the brown leather ski boots he recovered from German alpine troops after the war.

Mad River Glen was (and is) a skier's mountain ("Ski it if you can" is still their motto). It was a place with no frills. We usually stayed at Tucker Hill Lodge, built, owned, and run by another classmate of my father, Franny Martin. In those days, Mad River conducted an annual family ski race. The winner was determined based on times and, more importantly, on the number of combinations of skiers. With the exception of mother combinations, we had them all—father-son, father-daughter, sister-sister, brother-brother, and sister-brother. A Vermont family, whose name I have forgotten, had more combinations and for years were winners of the race. I remember the great satisfaction when we finally won and then kept the prize for the next year or so.

We went to Cannon Mountain a few times, staying in Franconia with the Hannahs. A second cousin of my father, Pauline White, had married one of skiing's legends, Seldon Hannah. Seldon Hannah skied for Dartmouth in the early 1930s and had been named to the 1940 Olympic team, but the games were cancelled because of the war. Pauline was also a very accomplished skier and an Olympic prospect, but contracted polio around 1940 and was confined to a wheelchair for the rest of her long life. Polly's Folly, one of the two steepest trails at Cannon, was named in her honor. Their daughter, Joan, skied in the 1960 Olympics at Squaw Valley and in the 1964 Olympics at Innsbruck.

~

By the mid 1960s, I began skiing less frequently, although I continued to ski every year. Marriage to a non-skier, children, and a tough stock market dominated the rest of that decade and much of the 1970s. Every

My father skiing at Temple Mountain, c. 1955

Me, c. 1957

year I would ski somewhere, usually in New Hampshire with family, and maybe once or twice out west. It wasn't until the later 1980s and early 1990s that I started skiing again more regularly; in the past several years I have skied between fifteen and twenty days each winter, half of that time out west. A change in equipment and skiing in the West have added new dimensions. New skis are shorter and more user-friendly, clothing is warmer, the bindings are easier to put on and safer, as are helmets, and the slopes in the West have more powder—bowls, on sunny days, are nirvana.

For the past several years I have taken, annually, a couple of trips to Vail with friends, both old and new. These trips mean a lot, not only because of the skiing, but also because of the camaraderie. Ten or eleven months go by between visits, yet conversation restarts remind me of the opening line from Oliver Wendell Holmes's *The Autocrat at the Breakfast Table*: "I was going to say, when I was interrupted. . . ." We ski hard; we laugh hard, and we wine and dine with great gusto.

Twenty or so years ago, one of my siblings came up with the idea of a family ski day at Mount Sunapee. It has become a wonderful tradition for a family, while not widely scattered from a geographical perspective, whose lives have taken different paths. We gather as the children of our father, talking of old days which each year are more distant, of a time when our responsibilities were none other than how many runs we could make, and of a time when the skiing community was much smaller and more intimate. Our skiing reunions themselves have now provided great memories. None of us who were there will ever forget the moment in 1996 when my older sister, Mary—who five years earlier had been diagnosed with breast cancer that had metastasized to her bones—become briefly airborne as she crossed a logging path while skiing down the Hansen Chase trail. Witnesses were concerned that her bones, grown fragile, would break if she fell; however, she landed on her feet, skied to the bottom, and with the exhilaration of an excited child, turned breathlessly toward us, "Did you see me take air?!"

In the past few years, my grandchildren have begun learning to ski. I watch with swelling pride in their developing improvement, as they ski down slopes with *élan* and determination. They are a marvel to witness.

~

A feature of skiing, perhaps unique in the sporting world, is that it is something one can do alone (although wiser with a friend) and one can do it for many years. Yet now that I'm in my seventies, age is something I think about. My skiing days will end when they end, but the memories I have accumulated will always be with me: hot chocolate and a doughnut in the warming hut at Whit's; a warm, spring day at Temple Mountain, skiing in shirt sleeves. Whenever I ski down the Lynx at Mount Sunapee, in my mind's eye I watch my father in his inimitable style, skiing while standing erect—I recall gate keeping at a veterans' race at Waterville Valley and him coming down the course, smoke curling from a pipe clenched in his teeth; entering the old lodge at the base of Sunapee, I see him speaking to other men wearing the insignia of the 10th Mountain Division. I see some of the giants, skiing pioneers like Joe Dodge, Seldon Hannah, Bob Livermore, and Al Sise, all of whom I met.

I think of the heaviness of rope tows on warm wet days and the chill when riding a single chair on a very cold day with a heavy blanket draped across my lap. I recall my early teens and the evening chore of replacing steel edges after a long day's skiing, and the wise-cracking on the bus ride back to Williston after a practice on Mt. Tom, with our coach, David Stevens. I remember gliding on my cross-country skis across the Back River in front of my house and over the marsh on a cold February day, and dropping into Genghis Kahn and skiing down the Slot, both at Vail, with powder up to my chest.

Seal skins, bamboo poles with baskets ten inches across, skijoring behind a horse on Middle Hancock Road, holding a rope as a "cat" pulled us up Pack Monadnock—all are memories I cherish. Those memories stretch back to that Christmas of 1944 in East River, Connecticut, when

With skiing pals at Vail, 2004

I walked around on my first pair of skis, and they reach forward to recent years, skiing with two granddaughters at Ski Sundown in northern Connecticut.

In that March issue of *The New Yorker,* Nick Paumgarten wrote of Fridtjof Nansen, a Norwegian who crossed Greenland on skis in 1888. He quotes Nansen: "It is better to go skiing and think of God than to go to church and think of sport." My sentiments exactly.

Family Reunions and the Miracle of Life

Come, speak to me of times gone by.
Remind me of our carefree youth.
Recall with me those nights we sang
And thought we knew the truth.

Susan Noyes Anderson
"Reflections on Another Day," 2003

IN AUGUST 2010, THE CHILDREN, GRANDCHILDREN, and great-grandchildren of my parents celebrated what would have been my father's one-hundredth birthday. We gathered at the Crane Estate in Ipswich, Massachusetts, built by Chicago plumbing magnate Richard T. Crane, Jr. The grounds are not far from Gloucester, where my parents met in 1936. The venue was the inspired choice of my sister Charlotte—and made one wish one's grandfather had gone into toilets.

The estate consists of 2,100 acres with a large house and a number of outbuildings. We took over the "casino" and what must have been at one point a guest cottage. The lawns roll east over two hummocks, and three- or four-hundred yards to a bluff from which one could look out onto salt marshes and the Atlantic Ocean.

The "casino" was most likely once a large party room for the young, where the noise from the carousing and the music would not have disturbed those in the main house; for us it was a place to serve a buffet lunch. Photos were taken; we walked to the bluffs. But best of all, better than lunch or the view, was the opportunity to visit with siblings, cousins, nephews, nieces, a plethora of in-laws, and a sprinkling of "significant others." I met many of the great-grandchildren for the first time.

My parents had nine children; from them came eighteen grandchildren, and now—if I have counted correctly—twenty-six great-grandchildren. It is startling to see what can happen over a few years if you leave a man and a woman alone for a few minutes!

My three sisters—Betsy, Charlotte, and Jenny—brought photos,

Grandmother Hotchkiss and family, 1956. I'm standing, fourth from the right.

My mother with her (then) twelve grandchildren, 1975

My Williams grandparents and their family, 1956—I'm second from right, back row

newspaper clippings, and an assortment of memorabilia, including a slide-show that Betsy set up of photos from my parents' childhood to the present, a wonderful cornucopia of lives lived and still being lived. My brother Frank brought copies of a recorded interview with my mother, taped two-and-a-half years before she died in 1990. (I brought 38.5 percent of the great-grandchildren!)

Although his life was cut short by cancer, my father's fifty-eight years saw remarkable change. The Wright Brothers piloted man's first flight seven years before he was born; less than a year after his death Neil Armstrong walked on the moon. My father was born during the halcyon days of the twentieth century's first decade, before the horrors of the trenches of World War I traumatized the world, and thirty years before the apocalypse that became World War II, a war in which he served. Above and beyond those experiences and his chosen work as a sculptor, he considered his most important contribution to be, as he wrote in a twenty-fifth reunion note for Harvard, his nine "ideas," the children he sired.

A family reunion makes one realize the marvel of life and the extraordinary odds against any individual being born. Not only did our parents have to meet, but so did every other ancestor going back to when life first evolved. And, not only did they have to meet, but the genesis of each of our lives depended upon a specific sperm meeting a specific egg—the odds of that happening has to be measured in the billions of trillions. The best description I have read that speaks to that miracle is a line from Tolstoy's *Anna Karenina*. It comes at the point when Levin's wife Kitty has just given birth. Levin observes, " . . . there at the foot of the bed, in the deft hands of Lizaveta Petrovna, like a small flame over a lamp, wavered the life of a human being who had never existed before and who, with the same right, with the same importance for itself, would live and produce its own kind."

This is the gift from our parents and it is why we honor them. Those of my generation have given the same to our children who, in turn, have given the same to theirs, and so on down through the years, in the continuum of life.

As my wife and I exited the grounds, winding down the drive past fields and copses, basking in the afternoon sun, the pleasure and comfort we'd felt at the reunion reaffirmed for us the importance of family as proof that life is truly a wonder, to be valued as something extraordinary, to be savored and to be lived to the fullest. We owe no less to those who created us.

The nine children, lined up by age in 1997, the last time we were all together:
George, Willard, Stuart, Jenny, Charlotte, Betsy, Frank, me, and Mary

Two Days in New Hampshire

THE TEMPERATURE WAS TWELVE DEGREES Fahrenheit as the chairlift reached the summit of Mount Sunapee in southern New Hampshire. The wind coming from the north, across the lake, added to the chill factor. Nevertheless, we were excited to be there and ready for the first run of the day.

For the past twenty-odd years, my siblings and I and our families—or at least some of us—have gathered at this mountain for a day of skiing. Tradition has confirmed the date to be the first Saturday in March. Mount Sunapee was selected as a place to reunite because it is easy for most of the family to reach, and, more importantly, because of the role it played in our growing up. Sunapee was where our father would take us for a taste of a "real mountain." In the early 1950s Sunapee had a single chairlift and a vertical drop of just over 1,000 feet, but it included two great trails for those of us who were older—Flying Goose and Lynx—and Chipmunk for the younger ones. Sunapee is not a large area, though it has expanded over the years, but it holds a host of memories and I greatly enjoy returning to the mountain. It occurs to me that I have been skiing there for nearly sixty years.

Since our father was an artist, he often would take us out of school so that we (and, of course, he) could ski on weekdays. With no lift lines we would ski hard all day. In my early teens, I recall racing on Flying Goose. Downhill races in those days had no control gates. He who made it from the starting gate to the finish line in the shortest period of time won the race. It did not take me long to realize that downhill racing and I were not a match.

A few years ago my sister Charlotte, her husband Fred Neinas, and I decided to go up a day early as a way to extend the reunion, but also as an excuse to get in an extra day's skiing. The three of us, along with an old friend, Hank Sykes, arrived Thursday evening at the Rosewood Country Inn in nearby Bradford. Friday dawned cold and windy, but the sun was bright. The wind had blown the loose snow off Upper Blast

Jenny and Charlotte, c. 1954

Off and Skyway Ledges, leaving the top of the trails hard-packed and a little icy. But below the ridgeline the packed powder provided a fast and smooth ride, fitting for the trails that are made for cruising. Four-and-a-half hours later, still exhilarated, we were tired and ready for a truly extraordinary dinner at The Inn at Pleasant Lake (owner-chef Brian Mackenzie presiding) in New London, New Hampshire.

On Saturday morning my sister Betsy and her husband Dick Moody joined us. Again, the conditions were wonderful with the weather warmer and the snow a bit softer. Skiing with Betsy is truly an experience. She has been coaching and instructing for most of her adult life. As a teenager she did a lot of racing, and she still skis with the power and grace of a down-hiller. By mid-morning it was obvious that any "losers" that day were those family members who had been unable to return to share the experience with us, but we hoped that the next year would see a record turnout. Driving back to Connecticut, to my non-skiing but understanding wife, I thought of how fortunate I am to come from such a large family, a family with whom I can spend an enjoyable two days skiing my heart out.

Remembering Memorial Day

The roses blossom white and red
On tombs where weary soldiers lie;
Flags wave above the honored dead
And martial music cleaves the sky.

Joyce Kilmer (1886–1918)[4]
The second stanza from "Memorial Day"

IT IS MEMORIAL DAY AROUND THE TIME I was ten or eleven that I remember best. In part, that is because memories of World War II seemed so recent, it having been concluded only six or seven years prior, and, in part, because a parade commemorating it in a small town is so personal. Out of 2,500 people in Peterborough, 341 (including my father) served in the armed forces during the Second World War—a remarkable number given that there could not have been many more than 400 eligible men in the town. (A few women served in the WAVES and WACS. However, the percentage of the population who served, 13.6%, was only slightly higher than the national average of 12.2%.) Thirteen of the men were killed; one of them, Theodore Reynolds, had a brother, Rodger, two grades above me. Another, Philip Sangermano, had a brother, Tony, with whom I used to ski at Whit's.

Many of the marines, sailors, and soldiers who served were men that I knew—Perkins and Robert Bass, Kenneth Brighton, Harley Cass, Paul Cummings, Milton Fontaine, Edward Lobacki, Elting Morison, and Walter O'Malley among others. Upon their return, most marched in the parade each year; a few, like my father, chose not to. Accompanying the soldiers and veterans were the high school band, composed of children older than I, but whose younger siblings I knew; along with Cub Scouts, Girl Scouts, and Boy Scouts. With several others on bicycles, we trailed the marchers to Pine Hill Cemetery, which lay just north of the village on Concord Street. It was a somber moment when, after the laying of

---

4 Kilmer was killed at the second Battle of the Marne.

a wreath, the sound of Taps could be heard, its haunting notes echoing from the hill beyond.

Of course I did not fully comprehend the symbolic significance of the tune, repeated year after year, nor the spine-tingling response it elicited, but I did realize that it represented a moment for the townspeople to annually pay tribute and say goodbye once again to those who had fallen in our nation's wars. I knew the moment was profound and rich in meaning.

Those of us who are fortunate to live in this country, either through birth or adoption, owe a debt of remembrance to those who gave their lives that the principles of democracy might endure. The signers of the Declaration of Independence promised to "mutually pledge to each other our Lives, our Fortunes and our Sacred Honor." We can do no less than recall that an estimated 1,200,000 have given their lives since 1776.

Originally called Decoration Day, Memorial Day, which was first celebrated in the years immediately following the Civil War, and Arlington National Cemetery, where more than 300,000 soldiers are buried, have come to symbolically represent all those who have fallen in our nation's wars. Each President, in his time, has participated in the Memorial Day ceremonies at Arlington. American flags are placed on the grave sites of all veterans, and a wreath is laid at the tomb of the Unknown Soldier.

My family's recent custom has been to observe a Memorial Day parade in the town of Old Lyme, Connecticut. Middle school and high school bands march, as do a fife and drum group from Deep River and a bagpipe brigade from New London. Scouts and Little League teams join them proudly. Antique cars, fire engines, and emergency medical service vehicles wind slowly up the street, joined by muscle cars—including a Ford Gran Torino and a Pontiac Trans Am from the early 1970s—that make their presence known with a roar of their engines. Local groups such as the Old Lyme Historical Society, the Lions Club, and the town's selectmen all drive or march toward the Duck River Cemetery where lie veterans from every war that has been fought on this continent and in distant lands, including those from colonial

Papa, 1944

campaigns such as King Philip's War. But the highlights are the veterans—some served in World War II and today are too old to march, others fought in Korea, Vietnam, the Gulf War, Iraq, and Afghanistan. Taps is played, as in Peterborough, and its echoes mix with the sound of the wind and of the cries of osprey flying overhead. It reminds us again of our eternal debt.

"The stockings were hung..." Christmas Eve, 1955

Bringing the Christmas tree home, December 24, 1950

Christmas Past and Present

It is a fair, even-handed, noble adjustment of things, that while there
is infection in disease, there is nothing so irresistibly contagious
as laughter and good-humor.

Charles Dickens (1812–1870)
A Christmas Carol (1843)

There is nothing sadder in this world than to awake
Christmas morning and not be a child.

Erma Bombeck (1927–1966)

IT IS A UNIVERSAL TRUTH THAT CHRISTMAS has become over
commercialized. At least, I have been known to argue that point.
However, the truth is that in my seventy-plus Christmases, there has
never been a time when commercialism and Christmas did *not* mix.
Importantly, what has remained unchanged is the magic that Christmas
conveys.

As children growing up in New Hampshire, we were not exposed
to the tree at Rockefeller Center, or the decorated stores along New
York's Fifth Avenue, as my children and our grandchildren have been.
But Derby's, Peterborough's department store, served just as well. The
warmth of the store was welcoming as one entered on a cold snowy day.
The sound of recorded Christmas carols filled the air. The aisles were
decorated with holly. Everything always looked clean and new. Living
four miles from the village, trips to town that did not involve school
were relative rarities, and a trip to Derby's was special.

In my memory, childhood Christmases run together, but what I remember best was how getting the tree on Christmas Eve and decorating
it and that night reading Clement Moore's *The Night Before Christmas*,
fueled anticipation for the next morning.

The late 1940s and very early 1950s had to have been a special time
for my parents and for the parents of most of my friends. World War II
was recently over and my parents, like so many, were thankful to have

Papa and the "Williams Ski Team," c. 1958

peace restored, vowing as others had done for countless generations that war would never infect their children. (Unfortunately, that vow never seems to be kept.) We lived on a small farm, as one might expect of young artists interested in living on their own while raising a large family. In those early years, the house lacked insulation and there was no central heating. While woodstoves heated the downstairs and the two bathrooms were heated with hot water from a coal-fired furnace, the bedrooms were very cold on winter nights.

We always got our tree on Christmas Eve. My father would hitch our horse Judy to a scoot and we would all hop aboard—by 1951, when I was ten, there already seven of us—and head for the woods. Once we'd located and chopped down a tree, we would return home, the bells on Judy's harness tinkling clearly, the vapor from her nostrils steaming in the cold clear air. The effort was worth it, as a fresh tree allowed my parents to use real candles to illuminate the branches.

With the tree set up and decorated, we hung our stockings alongside ones for the dogs, Mopsa and George. Later, just before we were sent off to bed, Mitzi our Shetland pony would come into the living room to

Merry Christmas

1956, back row: Charlotte, Betsy, Frank, Sydney
front row: Willard, Mary, George, Stuart, Jenny

hang one of her old horseshoes. That was always a special time, as my father would raise her front legs and the two would dance a jig.

Sleep never came easily on Christmas Eve, but try as we might we could never stay awake until midnight when, so we were told, Santa made his appearance. Nor were we ever able to confirm my mother's assertion that at midnight on Christmas Eve all the animals in the barn would converse in English. Instead, we would awake to the smell of coffee percolating and oatmeal that had been warming on the woodstove all night. Toast was made by salting the top of the stove and then placing slices of bread on it. Tears and laughter abounded, as we waited for all to assemble and walk single-file into the living room to see if Santa had truly arrived. He never failed us.

While those Christmases of yesteryear blur together, there are moments I recall clearly, like my maternal grandparents arriving from Madison, Connecticut, in 1946 and coming through the front door, which was rarely used. The memory is special, for my grandfather died the next year. I remember receiving my first Hardy Boys book, *The House on the Cliff,* by Fentin W. Dixon, when I was probably twelve. My

1963

excitement was such that I read it twice before letting my brother Frank read it once.

Thirty years later, our Christmases in Greenwich, Connecticut, continued the tradition of reading Clement Moore's wondrous tale, before a tree now decorated with electric lights. Stockings were hung as always, and a plate of cookies laid out on the hearth along with a glass of milk (that became beer, as our children grew older and their belief in Santa was maintained more to humor their parents). In the morning, which always arrived early, the plate and glass were empty.[5]

A recent Christmas Eve and Christmas morning spent at our daughter's home in Rye, New York, brought back many of my childhood memories, as well as memories of our children's youth. The Featherstons have central heating and there is no Shetland pony to hang her horseshoe, but the stockings were there and the magic of Christmas was alive and well, reflecting the excitement of children whose belief in Santa Claus has not diminished. The expressions of awe on the faces of our three grandchildren were as ageless as the tradition of Christmas. The holiday may reflect an overabundance of commercialism, but if that is the price we pay to keep the wonder that is childhood, it is cheap.

---

5 I remember once calling my mother at 7:30a.m. to tell her that the last present had been opened an hour earlier.

On Great-Grandparents

Our greatest responsibility is to be good ancestors.

Dr. Jonas Salk (1914–1995)

EACH OF US DESCENDS FROM EIGHT great-grandparents. As a sizable portion of our population immigrated from elsewhere, many people may not know the names of their great-grandparents. However, as all of mine were born in this country, and with the advent of that intrusive tool, the Internet, I have been able to learn something about most of them. Not surprisingly, there is more information available about the men than the women.

Great-grandparents precede us by almost exactly one hundred years; so it is easy to look back on the history of the time in which they lived. Mine were born between 1837 and 1854, meaning that they came of age in the pre- and post-Civil War eras. Their early adulthood coincided with the height of the Industrial Revolution. They were born just before and just after the Mexican War, as I was born in the early days of World War II. What the Vietnam War was to my generation, the Civil War was to theirs. And just as I missed having to fight in Vietnam, three of my four great-grandfathers escaped the battlefields of the Civil War. The fourth was too young to fight, but he was born in the South and he felt the effects of the war. In spite of the common tragedy of each war, the conflicts were entirely different. In terms of population, the country in 1861 was only one-sixth the size it was in 1965, yet Civil War deaths numbered ten times more than those in Vietnam. On the other hand, the battles of Antietam in 1862 and Gettysburg in 1863 were not broadcast live into our living rooms, like those of Khe Sanh and Hue in 1968.

The recession of the 1870s matched the recession that occurred during the 1970s. The Panic of 1907 presaged the Credit Collapse of 2008. And just as reforms followed the 1907 upheaval, including the creation of the Federal Reserve System and the trust-busting actions

Mary and Joseph Washington, c. 1880

of President Theodore Roosevelt, the credit collapse of 2008 is leading to similar reforms.

The twilight years of my great-grandparents were marked by World War I, and it seems likely that the War on Terror, assuming it lasts the decades suggested by some, will mark my last years.

A curious fact about my parents is that they were fifth cousins. This was not unusual in those early New England days. My mother and father shared great-great-great-great-grandparents: William Greenleaf and Mary Brown. William Greenleaf, born in 1725 and a merchant in Boston, was the high sheriff of Massachusetts' Suffolk County, which includes Boston, during the Revolutionary War. Mary Brown was the daughter of Judge Robert Brown of Plymouth, Massachusetts. Together they had thirteen surviving children, one of whom, Priscilla (born in 1755), married John Appleton of Salem; it is through them that my father descended. A second daughter, Rebecca, was born in 1766; she married Noah Webster (the lexicographer) who was then living in Hartford. It is through that line that my mother descended. It also means that my great-grandmothers Jane Appleton and Jane Louisa Fitch Trowbridge were third cousins.

All but one of my great-grandparents died many years before I was born. The one that survived the longest, Mary Bolling (Kemp) Washington, was the last to be born and likely suffered the most difficult childhood. She was born in Petersburg, Virginia, in 1854. She was seven when the Civil War began and ten during the siege of Petersburg. The siege, which deprived the inhabitants of sufficient food, lasted just over nine months, ending on March 25, 1865, about two weeks before General Lee surrendered at Appomattox, ninety-five miles to the west. While her parents died relatively young, my great-grandmother lived for ninety years, dying in 1944 when I was three; although I have no memory of her, I do have a cherished photograph of me on her lap, struggling to be free.

Of my four great-grandfathers, the one about whom I know the least is my namesake, Sydney Augustus Williams. He was born in Taunton, Massachusetts, on October 31, 1837, the son of Sydney Williams and Caroline (Messer) Williams. His mother was the daughter of Asa Messer, president of Brown University from 1804 to 1826. Sydney went to Bristol Academy in Taunton and graduated from Harvard College in 1858. Upon graduation he went to work in his father's insurance agency in Taunton and, at some point, became secretary of the American Mutual Insurance Company in Boston. In 1871 he married a widow, Charlotte Sullivan Blood (Richardson). She had been married to John Richardson and by him had two children. In 1873 she gave birth to my grandfather, Sydney Messer Williams, in Vevey, Switzerland. In 1965 my wife and I went to the city hall in Vevey and saw the record of his birth. My great-grandmother Williams died in 1896 and her husband died on January 26, 1912. An oil painting by a young Charlotte Blood of red flowers in a dark brown vase now hangs in my son Edward's home, reminding us that our ancestors are not just names on a piece of paper, but were real people who lived, breathed, and appreciated beauty.

My other paternal great-grandparents were also born in Massachusetts. Walter Hunnewell, the son of Horatio Hollis Hunnewell, a merchant banker, and Isabella Pratt Welles, was born in Boston on January 28, 1844. Walter graduated from Harvard in 1865. Before joining his father's firm (H. H. Hunnewell & Co.), he embarked as a volunteer and photographer on the Thayer Expedition, a trip up the Amazon led by Professor Louis Agassiz that lasted about a year.

Over time, Walter became a director of the Calumet and Hecla Mining Co., the Provident Institute for Savings, and the Webster & Atlas National Bank; he was a vice president of St. Mary's Mineral Land Co., and a trustee of Boston Lying-in Hospital, Peter Bent Brigham Hospital, the Massachusetts Horticultural Society, and other organizations. The "Italian Gardens" at "Wellesley," the house built by his father, flourished under Walter's eye when he inherited the estate in 1901, upon the death of his father at age ninety on May 20, 1901. Walter died on September 30, 1921.

On May 15, 1873, Walter married Jane Appleton Peele. Jane, born on December 8, 1848, was the daughter of Willard Peele and Sarah Ann Silsbee of Salem, Massachusetts. Sarah was one of eleven children—eight survived, including Edward Augustus Silsbee, a sea captain and noted collector of the poet, Percy Bysshe Shelley. (Edward Silsbee deserves a separate telling of his own story.[6] Jane gave birth to six children—one of whom, Willard, predeceased her—including my grandmother, Mary Peele Hunnewell. Jane died at age 44, on September 15, 1893, when my grandmother was seventeen.

My maternal great-grandparents represented the North and the South. My mother's paternal grandparents came from New Haven, Connecticut. My great-grandfather, Henry Lucius Hotchkiss, the sixth child of Henry Hotchkiss and Elizabeth Daggett Prescott, was born December 18, 1842, and married Jane Louisa Fitch Trowbridge in 1875. In 1843 the senior Henry, with his brother Lucius, had teamed up with L. Candee and formed a rubber manufacturing facility to produce rubber boots under the Goodyear license—the first company to utilize Charles

---

6 *The Aspern Papers*, the novella by Henry James (whose brother, William, accompanied Walter Hunnewell on the Thayer Expedition), is a fictionalized telling of an event in Edward Silsbee's life.

Walter Hunnewell with Mary and Walter, Jr., c. 1883

Goodyear's vulcanization process. By 1863, the elder Henry had become president of L. Candee, Inc. My great-grandfather (Henry Lucius) attended Hopkins Grammar School and Williston Academy in Easthampton, Massachusetts, (the school from which I graduated in 1959). He left Williston in 1860 to join his father in business. Henry Lucius's first job was paymaster of the New London Railroad, a company of which his father was a trustee. He soon joined L. Candee, Inc., and by 1863 was treasurer. By that time the company employed 2,000 people and was producing 20,000 boots and shoes a day. The senior Henry died in 1871, and Henry Lucius succeeded him as president of L. Candee & Co. as well as of The Union Trust Company, a New Haven bank founded in 1868. In 1892, L. Candee joined a few other independent

Henry Lucius Hotchkiss, c. 1895

rubber companies to form U.S. Rubber Company of New Jersey. My great-grandfather served as chairman and as a director before retiring in 1899 to take a trip around the world with his wife. He also was a director of the National New Haven Bank and a trustee of Hopkins Grammar School. He died at the age of eighty-seven on May 10, 1930, of a heart attack while attending the Harvard-Yale crew race on the Thames River in New London, Connecticut.

His wife, Jane Trowbridge, was the daughter (and fourth child) of Henry Trowbridge and Mary Webster Southgate, a granddaughter of Noah Webster.[7] Jane was born on November 16, 1851, in New Haven. She died on April 20, 1902, at the age of fifty. My grandfather was twenty-three at the time.

My mother's maternal grandparents lived in Tennessee. Her grand-

---

7 Mary's mother died giving birth to her; she was raised by her Webster grandparents. I have a letter from Noah Webster in which he refers to the upcoming nuptials between his granddaughter and Henry Trowbridge.

father was Joseph Edwin Washington and her grandmother was Mary Bolling Kemp. They lived on a farm called "Wessyngton" in Cedar Hill, Tennessee, about forty miles north of Nashville, not far from the Kentucky border. Joseph Edwin, born on November 4, 1851, was the son of George Augustine Washington and Jane Smith. George's father, Joseph, had acquired the land and built the house in the last decade of the eighteenth century. At its peak, the farm comprised about 15,000 acres and was the second-largest grower of dark fire-cured tobacco in the world— second to the Khedive of Egypt. During the Civil War, George made frequent trips to New York; his oldest son fled to Canada, so Joseph Edwin stayed home with his mother to defend the farm against Union raiders. After the war, Joseph Edwin graduated from Georgetown; three years later he graduated with the first class from Vanderbilt Law School. He was admitted to the bar, but never practiced. With his father, he managed the farm.

For two years he served as a representative to the state legislature and in 1887 was elected to Congress where he served ten years. Thus, my grandmother, born in 1888, spent her early years in Washington, D.C. In 1896 Joseph Edwin was appointed road commissioner for Robertson County where Wessyngton was located, and so returned to the farm. He was a director of the Nashville, Chattanooga & St. Louis and the Nashville & Decatur Railroads. In 1904 he became, along with two brothers-in-law, Felix Ewing and Charles Fort, a founding member of Planters Protective Association, an organization of dark-fired tobacco planters, organized against the so-called tobacco trust. He died August 28, 1915, and is buried in the family cemetery at Wessyngton.[8]

My great-grandmother, Mary Bolling Kemp, was born in 1854, the daughter of Judge Wyndham Kemp and Seignora Peyton Bolling, in Petersburg, Virginia. Petersburg, of course was the site of the infamous

---

8 Wessyngton remained in the family until the early 1980s. At that point ownership resided with my mother, her three brothers, and four cousins. As none of them lived in Tennessee, it became impractical to keep it; the cemetery, however, remains.

My great-grandmother, Mary Kemp Washington, and me, 1941

siege in the last months of the Civil War. During those months, Robert E. Lee's son, Fitzhugh, became a life-long family friend and later became godfather to my grandmother, Elizabeth Wyndham Washington. Mary Kemp, after a difficult early life in Petersburg during the siege, bore four children, including my grandmother, and lived to the age of ninety, dying in 1944; she is buried alongside her husband at Wessyngton. The photograph of my great-grandmother with me on her lap is a reminder that the Civil War is not all that distant.

The historian, Margaret MacMillan, in her book, *Dangerous Games,* warns of those who use history to justify their interpretation of events. However, history does help us see our lives in a larger context. Edward Hallett Carr, in his 1961 lecture, "What is History," said that history is "an unending dialogue between the present and the past." Jessica DuLong, in her delightful book, *My River Chronicles,* writes: "Grasping history's messages is more intuitive than literal, but the information connects us to our place in time." And, while I am not a fan of ancestor worship, I do think we benefit from knowledge of whence we came. As much as we are products of our environment, equally we are a result of the genetics we have inherited. I have found the study of one's family to be meaningful in understanding the continuum of history. We recognize the miracle that has allowed us to be born—a function of two strangers meeting, falling in love, and having children. It is a never-ending procession toward infinity, both exciting and humbling.

A Letter on V-J Day

To my brothers and sisters:

On August 14, 1945, Mama drove her four children from Peterborough to Nashua (I believe, although it could have been Manchester) to pick up Papa who was returning from service in Italy. The day constitutes one of my earliest memories. I recall the honking of car horns, the waving of hands, lights flashing, as we drove the twenty or so miles. The exhilaration was palpable, even to a four-and-a-half-year-old. I remember the troop train arriving, and then Papa coming toward us and us rushing toward him.

The emotions of relief and joy my parents associated with this reunion had to have been stronger than anything I can imagine. Literally millions upon millions of people had died, including more than 600,000 Americans, over the previous six years. That my father had survived, unscathed, must have seemed miraculous.

Driving back to Peterborough we stopped at a field between Milford and Wilton—across a small metal bridge—for a picnic, whether lunch or supper I do not recall.

As I think back on that day, I realize that the war ended prematurely because of the dropping of two atomic bombs in Japan (in Hiroshima on August 6 and in Nagasaki on August 9), killing close to 300,000 civilians—an almost incalculable tragedy. Yet I am glad that Truman authorized the use of atomic weapons. Had he not, most certainly the United States would have staged the planned October invasion of the Japanese mainland. The official Allied estimates assumed a million casualties, most of whom would have been Americans. When Papa left Italy in late July to sail home, his division was expected to be part of that landing force. He was only expecting to be home for a month's leave before heading west to train for the invasion. His unit was on their ship when they received the news of Japan's impending surrender, which meant peace and life for so many.

In the last letter Papa sent Mama from Colorado, as he was being mustered out of the service, he wrote, "I become more and more surprised that I ever lived through it at all. There would have been very few of us left if it lasted any longer."

V-J Day is a day we should all remember and one for which we should all be thankful. Every time somebody raises the question of the morality of Truman's decision, think of Papa's words.

Love, Sydney

Fifty Years of Marriage

*"What counts in making a happy marriage is not so much how
compatible you are, but how you deal with incompatibility."*

Leo Tolstoy (1828–1910)

APRIL 11, 2014, MARKED OUR FIFTIETH wedding anniversary.
It is a good long time. None of our parents made it this far. Death
intervened.

During the past fifty years we have been homeless (early in our marriage, we hung out at Caroline's parents' apartment in New York for six
months) and have had seven residences, eight if you include a boarding
house that became home for a couple of months in late 1965.

We were married before I finished college, a quaint concept in today's world of thirty-something marriages and two incomes, but not
uncommon in those prehistoric days. Marriage is viewed differently
today. For one thing, people marry later. The population of the United States has increased 58 percent since 1964, while weddings are up a
mere 23 percent. On the other side of the ledger, the divorce rate is up
130 percent. It makes one wonder: Does wisdom diminish with age?

Other facts, while irrelevant to the subject of fifty years of marriage,
are of interest. Gross Domestic Product during those years increased
twenty-three times, while the Dow Jones Industrial Average is up about
twenty-one times. In 1964, Lyndon Johnson was in the White House and
Vietnam was just beginning to heat up. A first-class stamp cost a nickel.
Civil Rights marchers were murdered in Mississippi. Northern Dancer
won the Kentucky Derby and the Beatles appeared on the Ed Sullivan
show. If it seems like the distant past, that's because it is.

I met Caroline on New Year's Eve 1961 at a now defunct ski area in
southern New Hampshire called Temple Mountain; we were introduced
by my sister, Mary. We saw each other that evening and within a matter of weeks knew we wanted to marry. I was twenty-one at the time.

March 11, 1962, the day I asked Caroline to marry me

Two-and-a-half months after meeting her, while in a ski lodge in North Conway, New Hampshire, I asked Caroline to marry me; she accepted. A few hours later she broke her leg on Wildcat Mountain during what would prove to be her last trip down hill on skis. (She had broken an ankle skiing each of the prior two years.)

We grew up very differently, Caroline on Park Avenue in New York and I on a little farm in a small town in New Hampshire. But we were not quite as different as might first appear. For example, both of our fathers had Harvard in common; Caroline's father graduated from the law school and mine from the college. Caroline had friends in Boston, where she was then living, whose parents were friends of my parents. Nevertheless, the differences were quite obvious. The sidewalks of New York differ from the rocky fields and pastures of New Hampshire. To enjoy the outdoors meant a trip to Central Park for Caroline, while I would saddle a horse and take off over miles of dirt roads. My wife had

Our wedding day, April 11, 1964

Caroline and me, October 2012

only to step outside to enjoy the cultural advantages of New York, from Broadway to the Museum of the City of New York, from the Stork Club to the Metropolitan Opera. In Peterborough we had the MacDowell Colony, the Guyette Museum, and, during the summer, the Peterborough Players. Caroline's family always had a dachshund, while mine had several dogs of varying breeds that lived alongside cats and a barn full of horses, goats, chickens, and two peacocks. I was one of nine children while Caroline had one brother.

Following college, and before the start of my first "real" job, we took $2,000 and went to Europe for eleven weeks. We had rooms booked in Paris for the night we arrived and for the night before we left. The other seventy-five nights we left to chance. Arthur Frommer's *Europe on Five Dollars a Day*, a rented Volkswagen bug, a map, sleeping bags, some travelers cheques (no credit cards), and a couple of small suitcases were our sole companions. It proved to be a great time, and making the trip after almost a year of marriage—we celebrated our first wedding anniversary in Vienna—proved fortuitous. The physical attraction, while still exciting, was no longer all-consuming, so we were able to get to know one another far better and become friends as well as lovers.

In 1974, three years following our move to Greenwich, Connecticut, with three small children and seven years after I entered the securities business, Wall Street went into a severe bear market. It had been a long time coming. The Dow Jones Average neared 1,000 in early 1966, and in the intervening eight years, it fell, rose, fell, and rose, but in 1974 stocks went to twelve-year lows. On May 1, 1975, fixed commissions were abandoned in favor of negotiated rates (a plan that ultimately proved very positive, but at the time was devastating) and the commission business slowed markedly. With two children in private schools and a third in the wings, and a mortgage on a house beyond our means, our marriage suffered a strain. There were moments when I—and I'm sure Caroline, too—sympathized with the lines of Neil Lindores' uncle in Andrew Greig's *The Return of John Macnab*:

"How ill advised it was, and rash, to start upon this foolish dash!"

My income virtually disappeared; we were forced to sell the house off Round Hill Road, send a couple of horses and goats to my mother in New Hampshire, and move to another house with less land about two miles away on Lake Avenue. But financial hardship brought determination and reinforced our marriage. The 1974 recession caused a lifestyle change, not only for us, but for others on Wall Street. In the early 1970s I would drop the children at school and catch the 7:40a.m. train to New York, arriving at the office a few minutes before 8:30a.m.—a leisurely pace. The train was crowded and reflected life on Wall Street in those halcyon days. However, it wasn't long before the 6:00a.m. train became the train of choice for me and for hundreds of commuters. Being at your desk by 7:00a.m. became the norm. The children took the bus to school.

The years went by; the children grew and flourished. Wall Street recovered and I was fortunate to find work that I enjoyed and that treated me well.

The focus of Caroline's attention has been, since our eldest was born, on the children. She has showered them with love, provided practical advice to their inquiries; she has acted as a sounding board to them. They have been her *raison d'être*.

Within a year of one another, our children all married. Once the three of them set up their own homes, our lives reset themselves to the freedom of the years before children, giving us time for new discoveries. However, after three years our children began producing their own families and now the grandchildren are the fortunate beneficiaries of Caroline's love and wisdom. I revel in the love they bestow on her. My admiration grows and the foundation of our marriage becomes stronger.

There is no moral or lesson in this short essay. It is almost impossible to foretell whether a marriage will work or not. A lot has to do with luck. Certainly, marriage is something that needs attention. Compassion, respect, understanding, and, of course, love play big roles. One partner may be the counselor on Monday and the counselee on Tuesday. Staying married does not necessarily make one a better person. Two very fine people may find themselves incompatible and the best course may prove to be divorce. I revert to my earlier premise: Luck plays a big role. Caroline and I have been fortunate and we know it. There have been times of angst. There have been moments of doubt, but happiness and satisfaction have dominated. The decision to marry involves a bet on the very long term. We both realize the role of coincidence—had we not met when we did our lives might have taken very different paths. Those paths might well have led to happiness, but the question of "what if?" is not one that consumes us. We did meet. We were young and took a chance. It worked.

With our grandchildren, October 2012

Williston Ski Team, 1958, me in the center, two coaches on the right

Fiftieth Reunion—Williston '59

"And now I can't wait; they've set the date;
Our fiftieth is coming, I'm told.
It should be a ball, they've rented a hall
At the Shady Rest Home for the old."

Author Unknown

SHAVING EVERY MORNING, the face in the mirror has aged without my noting. My hair, once dark, turned gray then white. Lines appeared where none existed. Brown spots surfaced, initially unnoticed, not to mention unwanted. How pertinent seem the words from *My Fair Lady*, "I've grown accustomed to your looks, accustomed to your voice, accustomed to your face."

So, in many respects, attending my fiftieth high school reunion in 2009 was a shock. Those seventeen- and eighteen-year-old faces, etched in memory from fifty years ago, and recalled in a recent perusing of my yearbook, had morphed into strange and elderly visages. The sensation had to have been similar to that experienced by Dorian Gray when, in the attic of his house, he discovered the painting of himself—the painting in which the portrait had aged while he had remained eternally young.

The weekend, though, proved more enjoyable than I expected. Being exceptionally immature at the time I attended Williston, I never took advantage of the privilege and opportunity the school offered and so had been disinclined to return to the place from which I garnered so little and gave even less. However, what I discovered was a coterie of classmates who had grown into mature and pleasant men. Gone were the cliques of the past—the jocks, the nerds, the preppies, and the hoods—along with the competitiveness that marks younger men in their prime. Instead I found aging gentlemen, many of whom have had fascinating careers and lives, but all of whom radiated a sense of achievement and inner happiness.

At one point, as we were jostled together for yet another round of photos, I was almost overcome by the magnitude of fifty years. It is a long time. Fifty years after the Continental Congress declared "that these colonies are, and of Right ought to be, Free and Independent States," the United States was under the leadership of its sixth democratically elected president. Fifty years following the silencing of the guns at Appomattox, sixty thousand British troops died in the first three days of the Battle of the Somme.

The fifty years following our graduation from Williston have been a remarkable period. We have had eleven Presidents, from Eisenhower, who was old enough to have been our grandfather, to Barack Obama, who is young enough to be our son. The population of the United States has almost doubled during those years—from 180,000,000 to 330,000,000; living standards have risen concurrently, giving lie to the doomsayers of the Club of Rome. The Dow Jones Industrial Average rose from 629.97 on June 6, 1959, to 8763.10 on June 6, 2009—a compounded return of 5.4 percent before dividends. We have known nine recessions, but far more years of economic growth. We have stood in gas lines, and dealt with the twin concerns of high inflation and high interest rates. We underwent the soul-searching years following the war in Vietnam, and have benefitted from the bountiful results of the Reagan Revolution.

We have witnessed a race for space that began in the fall of our junior year, when the Soviets launched Sputnik 1 on October 4, 1957; twelve years later, in time for our tenth reunion, America became the first nation to put a man on the moon. Our country fought and lost an unpopular war in Vietnam at the cost of 58,000 lives. We successfully pushed the dictator of Iraq back after his invasion of Kuwait. We were attacked by Islamic terrorists on 9/11, an act which altered our country and divided our citizens, but highlighted those liberties we take for granted and reminded us of the fragility of our democracy and of our individual mortality. We read of the murder of untold thousands in China as the Cultural Revolution began and then ended coincident with the death of Mao Tse Tung. The Berlin Wall was erected in 1961 shortly after our graduation and fell twenty-eight years later—at the time of our thirtieth anniversary—as the forces of democracy and capitalism defeated the tyranny and repression of Communism, providing freedom and opportunity to millions of Eastern Europeans.

Great strides have been made in the social fabric of the nation. The Civil Rights struggles were a part of our young manhood. At the time we graduated, segregation was the rule in the South: African-Americans were made to drink from separate water fountains and to sit at the back of busses; they were not permitted to attend many schools in the South. Yet, in time for our fiftieth reunion, we elected as president our first African-American. Women, who were denied opportunities in the workplace and prevented from attending many educational institutions, have made great strides toward equality. Three of the last four secretaries of State have been women, one of them also an African-American. And in 2007, a woman was elected Speaker of the House of Representatives, the third highest office in America. Democracies have mushroomed around the world, more than tripling in the past fifty years. Communications and the Internet have changed our lives in ways inconceivable at the time of our graduation. The advantages many of us had growing up are now offered to an ever-increasing multitude.

Reunion weekend was an opportunity to look back on the passage of half a century and to consider the age we are now. It was sobering to note the appearance of a tent for those celebrating their twenty-fifth and fiftieth anniversaries, but none for the seventy-fifth. At a moving memorial service on Saturday, the names of those graduates who had died in the past year were read aloud. It had been forty-five years since I attended a reunion and fifty years since I had seen most of my classmates. As I heard the names of those of the class of 1959—Bill Ellis, David Westgate, and John Willett—men whom I had not seen in fifty years, their faces appeared in my mind as they had been, forever young. As in A. E. Housman's *Athlete*, the name did not die before the man.

A welcome addition to the usual nametag was a photo of each of us, recovered from the dusty pages of our yearbook, so, looking at a classmate, one was able, at a glance, to see both the past and the present. Concerns regarding the passage of time and the natural alteration of our bodies gave way to conversations about lives lived well, families loved and expanding, jobs that brought satisfaction, travels that educated, and, for several, well-earned retirement. While old school tales, embellished of course, of youthful indiscretions were enjoyed, enough time had passed, so that most of the conversation dealt with other subjects, of the present and the future. Thankfully, medical problems and politics were generally avoided. It was like meeting a group of men and their wives for the first time, but knowing we had something in common in our distant past. The fact that we are no longer encumbered or intimidated by the role our fellow students once played—the best actor, the top student, or the foremost athlete—provided the means for familiar and comfortable conversation.

I had not looked forward to the weekend, but as Caroline and I drove home following dinner on Saturday we spoke of the day and a half, and of the pleasure we derived from spending time with an enjoyable group, importantly ones I had known in their teens and now, in the late summer of their years, ones with whom I am reacquainted. My old roommate, John Harper, had urged me to attend. Thanks, John.

On Turning Seventy

"I don't feel old. I don't feel anything until noon. Then it's time for my nap."

Bob Hope (1903–2003)

THE MOST REMARKABLE THING about turning seventy, other than the veneration one expects but rarely gets, is how unremarkable it all seems. Of course, there is significance to aging—one is supposed to be revered for one's sagacity and respected for one's endurance. Old age is associated with patinas, such as one might find on a dusty volume, an antique chair or, better yet, in a fine Bordeaux. But when I turned seventy I didn't feel any more revered or respected (other than by my grandchildren whose powers of discernment are not yet fully developed) than I did a week before.

Gertrude Stein once said, "We are always the same age inside." That is true. I look at my wife, or my brothers and sisters, and I see the person I knew fifty or more years ago. Returning to my high school's fiftieth reunion a few years ago, it was not the wrinkled, stooped, balding, elderly gentlemen that confronted me that I noticed; it was the young men they had been. Looking at myself in the mirror every day for the roughly 10,000 times I have shaved, I never notice the gradual change in my features. I feel a little like Dorian Gray, unaware there is an aging portrait in the attic.

As much as anything, it is the rapidity with which time seems to sail by, that is most notable. Thoughts of mortality rise to the surface more frequently than they did twenty or thirty years ago. In my teens I thought I was immortal, but no longer. Thornton Wilder captured the fleetness of time in his play, *Our Town*, written in Peterborough, when he was a resident of the MacDowell Colony. The play is an allegory; it traces the residents of a small New England village through several generations. The stage manager delicately and sensitively assists the viewer through several scenes portraying critical moments in the lives of some of the residents, from birth to marriage to death. In the middle of the second act—on Emily Webb's and George Gibb's wedding day—the stage manager ruminates on Mr. and Mrs. Gibb's life together: "You know how it is: You're twenty-one or twenty-two and you make some decisions; then *whissh!* You're seventy." That is the way I feel, especially about the passing of the years since I met my wife, Caroline.

Life is filled with decisions. We pick a college. We find a place to live. We get married and have children. We pick up and move. We change careers. Each decision carries consequences, most of which cannot be foreseen. Decisions, subsequent to mine, have resulted in ten grandchildren, a source of immense pleasure and enormous pride. Knowing that they will follow fills me with hope for a future that too often appears uncertain. The message is: Life is filled with wonder and surprises; it cannot be foreseen; it must be savored. The greatest regret we have as we age is rarely what we did, but the things we might have done, but did not.

In a speech in 1905, on the occasion of his seventieth birthday, Mark Twain said, "Three score and ten! It is the Scriptural statute of limitations." I don't think so. Seventy today is not the same as in my grandfathers' day. I cannot picture my grandparents schussing Vail's Riva Ridge, as I recently did. When I go out on the tennis courts at the Hillsboro Club in Florida, I look and feel like a newborn gazelle. There are people in their nineties batting the ball back and forth with surprising vigor. The concept of retiring is unappealing and, in fact, frightening, marking as it does the end of a person's active life. It would bring to an end a career I still enjoy. The business has brought great friendships, for which I am thankful; to be surrounded with youth helps keep me young.

Henry Wadsworth Longfellow wrote: "To be seventy years old is like climbing the Alps. You reach a snow-crowned summit, and see behind you the deep valley stretching miles and miles away, and before you other summits higher and whiter, which you may have the strength to climb or not. Then you sit down and meditate and wonder which it will be."

October 2012

While I enjoy the memories, I don't have to sit down and meditate about the future. I know that I will aim for the "higher and whiter" summits, and will continue to live this life and hike these hills as long as I am able.

Christmas card, 2013

We Are All Kin

WE SPEND HOURS IN TRIVIAL PURSUIT and too little time on meaningful issues. At a time when forty-seven million Americans are on food stamps, 10.4 million people are unemployed, our nation's debt has been growing exponentially and stateless terrorists are stalking people around the globe, we are fixated on ensuring that the Little Sisters of the Poor can receive morning after pills, folks in Colorado can smoke marijuana, and those in New York cannot sip twenty-ounce soft drinks. We worry about issues over which we have little control, like spotted owls and polar icecaps, while ignoring complex issues like understanding what it means, in a civil society, to live freely under the rule of law. We want to please everyone and, consequently, too often please no one. Leaders in politics and the media concentrate on issues that divide us, rather than on those that unite us.

At the same time, we forget how insignificant we are and how large the world is. And we pay too little attention to the remarkable chain of events that had to occur in order that we might be here. The mathematical odds against any one of us being born are overwhelming. We are lucky to live in this age and even more fortunate to live in a free country.

Every person is unique, yet we all came from the same place—out of Africa. While no one knows how many of our ancestors left Africa and over what time periods, the consensus believes they left in waves, beginning more than 60,000 years ago. From those common ancestors was born the human race as we know it. Compared to an average human lifespan of eighty or so years, 60,000 years is a long time, but on a planet that is 4.5 billion years old, 60,000 years barely registers.

Ancestry is fascinating, and history is more meaningful when we associate it with a parent, grandparent, or great-grandparent. For example, President William Howard Taft is not widely remembered, but was president when my father was born in 1910. Ulysses S. Grant was president in 1873 when my paternal grandfather was born, and Martin

Van Buren was president at the time of my paternal great-grandfather's birth, in 1837, just over a hundred years before my own arrival.

When we look at our lineage through the lens of compounded returns we reach the inevitable conclusion that we are all related. In a recent "Sunday Review" section of *The New York Times*, A.J. Jacobs wrote of his estimated 75 million "cousins," a group for whom he admits not buying birthday gifts! While his numbers sound far-fetched, they are not. We each have two parents, four grandparents, and eight great-grandparents. The number from whom we descend doubles each generation, stretching back to the beginning of time. If we assume three generations per century and go back to the time of the Norman Conquest, or just under 1,000 years ago (and using the same mathematical exercise we associate with Warren Buffett), each of us would have descended from 536,870,912 twenty-seven-great grandparents. The problem is that there are 7 billion of us today and there were only 300 million in the year AD 1000, according to estimates by the United Nations Department of Economic and Social Affairs. If we had all descended from unique ancestors, the earth's population should have been 3.5 quintillion in the year 1066. Obviously, we must all be related.

In my family, we have been able to trace some of our ancestors. For example, my siblings and I have at least one set of great-great-great-great-great grandparents common to both my mother's and my father's sides. William Greenleaf was appointed Sheriff of Suffolk County (Boston) in 1776 by the Provincial Congress. He and his wife Mary Brown had fifteen children, two of whom died as infants and a third at the age of eighteen. (The one who died at eighteen, Stephen, was a student of medicine and surgery at Harvard and died of a fever contracted when working aboard a prison ship in Boston Harbor.) One daughter, Priscilla, married John Appleton, from whom my father descended. A younger daughter, Rebecca, married Noah Webster, my mother's great-great-great grandfather. In all, the Greenleafs' surviving children produced eighty-five grandchildren.

One of my high school friends, Tom Korson, is also descended from the Greenleafs, so he is my sixth cousin, something we never knew when at school. Sorry, Tom, but being a descendant of William Greenleaf is no big deal. A quick calculation would estimate that the Greenleaf's descendants, in the succeeding ten generations, would number somewhere between half a million and five million—and very possibly more. Intermarriages, childhood diseases, and the Civil War may have reduced those numbers, while larger families would have increased them. Whatever the number, Great-great-great-great-great Grandpa Greenleaf would not be able to pick me out of a line-up, and he is only marginally important in my life, as he was simply one of 128 great-great-great-great-great grandparents I have.

As an indication of the power of compounded returns when it comes to families and descendants, I was asked about twenty-five years ago by a friend who was involved with the Mayflower Society of New York if I might hazard how many people living in New York State could trace their heritage to the Mayflower. Taking what I assumed was a wildly bullish guess, I said about 100,000. He told me that the Society's estimate was seven million, or a third of the population of the State. I was flabbergasted until I started doing the math. There were 102 passengers plus a crew of twenty on the Mayflower. About half died the first winter. The remaining crew sailed for England in the spring. Because of the laws of compounding, the numbers become very big when we go back fourteen or so generations. Assume that thirty-five of the survivors had children. Further assume that for the first four generations each had four surviving children, the next five generations had three children, and the last four had two children. Those calculations would produce 34,836,480 across the country in fourteen generations—a lower estimate than that produced by the Mayflower Society in the 1980s. If one assumed that my grandparents' and my parents' generations had three surviving children each, there would be 78,383,080 Mayflower descendants, more than twenty percent of the U.S. population. Conclusion: Despite pretensions to the contrary, there is nothing very exclusive about the Mayflower Society.

Regardless of our mixed heritage, politicians like to place us in discrete compartments: Hispanic-Americans, Asian-Americans, or African Americans, for example. But that is misleading. We are not Blacks, Caucasians, Asians, or Latinos. We are Americans. We are segregated for political purposes. And politicians do it not just by race, but by creed, gender, age, sexual orientation, and now by wealth and income. This practice is divisive and serves no purpose other than political expediency.

Pride in one's nominal heritage is understandable and should be celebrated. Parades and festivities like St. Patrick's Day, and Puerto Rican, Jewish, and Greek heritage days are an important part of our culture. Nevertheless, we should never forget we are all members of the human race and we Americans are citizens of a great nation whose melting pot reflects the commonality of our ancestry.

In the late 1950s and early 1960s, during the Civil Rights movement, my paternal grandmother—a woman who spent six years at MIT—told me that at some future time all humans would be of one color. Racial differences, she believed, would disappear. She is right, but "eventually" is a long a time. Politics should be color-blind *today*. Politicians (and much of the media) divide us because they find it more convenient to address the specific needs of a specific group. Doing so makes for expedient political advantage. It avoids having to discuss the broader issues of what it would mean to live in a society where freedom is suppressed. Ideas are far more important than physical characteristics or personal preferences. It is the ability to think that differentiates us from other animals. The concepts of freedom and the rule of law, the role of religion in society, and the meaning of justice are the issues we should be debating. And we should never stop doing so.

While unanimity in what we have in common as members of the human race is good, unanimity in ideas suggests a population that has stopped thinking for itself—like the Eloi of H.G. Wells' *The Time Machine*. A gridlocked Congress encourages blame. And blame substitutes for debate. There is a tendency among the media, and with many politicians, to look upon failure to enact legislation as a negative manifestation of our political system. It is not. People operating in free markets do things. Governments set the boundaries and act as referee.

The critical element of a democracy is the ability to express one's opinions. A society that freely debates issues is open. A society that condemns specific groups, or vilifies others is closed. It is on the differences in political philosophies that our discourse should be focused, not on the color of our skin, our gender, our religion, or the country from which our ancestors hailed. After all, we are kin.

August, 1944. Left to right: Frank, Mary, Mama holding Betsy, Papa, and me

Afterword

THE GREATEST PLEASURE I DERIVED in putting together this collection came from the memories I was able to relive. It made me feel how lucky I have been, to have been born when I was and raised how I was. More importantly, I recognize that my fortune found its true North Star when I found the woman who would become my wife. My luck continued in the three children she bore and the ten grandchildren that have followed.

I understand what Ralph Waldo Emerson meant when he began an essay on history:

> *There is no great and no small,*
> *To the Soul that maketh all:*
> *And where it cometh, all things are,*
> *And it cometh everywhere.*
> *I am the owner of the sphere,*
> *Of the seven stars and the solar year,*
> *Of Caesar's hand and Plato's brain,*
> *Of Lord Christ's heart, and Shakespeare's strain.*

The word "history" derives from the Greek, *historia*, which means learning by asking. Toward the end of the essay, Emerson writes: "History no longer shall be a dull book. It shall walk incarnate in every just and wise man. . . . The idiot, the Indian, the child and unschooled farmer's boy, stand nearer to the light by which nature is to be read, than the dissector or the antiquary."

While we live in the present and must prepare for the future, history is always fascinating and, to me, best understood when we can associate people with periods of time. For those of us lucky enough to be able to trace our ancestry back, it is much easier to consider the Civil War period if we associate it with someone from whom we are descended that lived in that time. For my grandchildren and their children, I hope that they, when they study the latter half of the twentieth century, will be able to place the great events of that time in context of this one boy's life.

Many of these pieces were written while looking back sixty and more years, to a time when I was the age of my grandchildren today. They are a reminder, I hope, that the past is never completely lost.

Old Lyme, Connecticut
April 2014

ACKNOWLEDGMENTS

LIKE MOST THINGS IN LIFE, this book is a collaborative effort. Many people have been instrumental in the writing these essays.

First, I want to thank Andy Monness, Neil Crespi, and Herb Hardt for putting up with my scribblings when I should have been doing something more productive. More importantly, I appreciate their kindness and encouragement. Andy has known my family for over fifty years; so his insights were invaluable. Neil's quest for perfection and single-minded pursuit of goals are traits I hope have rubbed off on me and may be manifested in these pages. Herb's knowledge of English and grammar far exceeds mine, and, despite his greater size and his military background, he was always gentle in his admonitions.

Sarah Bauhan of Bauhan Publishing in Peterborough has known my family for years and took riding lessons from my mother years ago. In agreeing to publish these essays, she placed her firm at risk in associating with one such as me. Mary Ann Faughnan took on the herculean task of editing my untutored scribblings, literally creating a silk purse from a sow's ear. Henry James had the job of designing the wonderful cover and placing the photographs, which remind me of a time that seems so distant that it must have belonged to someone else.

To my brothers and sisters—Frank, Betsy, Charlotte, Jenny, Willard, and George—I owe a great deal of gratitude. You answered questions. You told me when my memory was faulty. You remembered things that were at best only vague, uncertain dreams. If only my memory were as good as it seemed when reeling off incidents that happened more than sixty years ago. I also want to thank my sister Mary and brother Stuart who did not live to see this book, but who were (and are) critical to its birth.

My children, Sydney, Linie, and Edward, have always been what every parent desires—loving, smart, and caring. Between them, they with their spouses—with whom Caroline and I are equally blessed—are cultivating a great crop of grandchildren. They will be maturing over the next couple of decades into citizens who will keep our country productive, youthful, and competitive.

Lastly, I want to thank my wife Caroline, without whom none of this would have happened—the children, the grandchildren, not even the essays. She has stood by me for over fifty years and remains as dear to me as when we married in April 1964. The memories we have shared are of incalculable value. I look forward to many more years of good times.